D1560052

Cogito?

ß

COGITO?

Descartes and Thinking the World

Joseph Almog

OXFORD
UNIVERSITY PRESS
2008

OXFORD
UNIVERSITY PRESS

Oxford University Press, Inc., publishes works that further
Oxford University's objective of excellence
in research, scholarship, and education.

Oxford   New York
Auckland   Cape Town   Dar es Salaam   Hong Kong   Karachi
Kuala Lumpur   Madrid   Melbourne   Mexico City   Nairobi
New Delhi   Shanghai   Taipei   Toronto

With offices in
Argentina   Austria   Brazil   Chile   Czech Republic   France   Greece
Guatemala   Hungary   Italy   Japan   Poland   Portugal   Singapore
South Korea   Switzerland   Thailand   Turkey   Ukraine   Vietnam

Published by Oxford University Press, Inc.
198 Madison Avenue, New York, New York 10016

www.oup.com

Oxford is a registered trademark of Oxford University Press

Library of Congress Cataloging-in-Publication Data
Almog, Joseph.
Cogito? : Descartes and thinking the world / Joseph Almog.
p.   cm.
Includes index.
ISBN 978-0-19-533771-6
1. Descartes, René, 1596–1650.   2. Thought and thinking.   I. Title.
B1875.A487 2007
128'.3—dc22
2007023072

1 3 5 7 9 8 6 4 2
Printed in the United States of America
on acid-free paper

Dedicated to Serge Lang and Keith Donnellan

Preface

Cogito should be the last proposition in one's repertoire to engender a question mark.* What is this question mark doing then? Is there any question–doubt–uncertainty about my...thinking? Is this not, as Descartes likes to say, the "Archimedean point" of my (cognitive) life? My students often complain with impatience that, by wondering in this Cogito? vein, I confront them with another one of those invented philosophical problems. What in the world could be the problem about thinking, since we do it all the time, we live by it?

We do do it—thinking—all the time. But we should not be so sure that it is in the world that we do it, at least not the real world of kicking soccer balls and eating ice cream. The elusiveness of thinking has made many philosophies to account for it by making it an act outside and, often, against nature, an act whose direct object—unlike the objects of kicking and eating—is sublimated, an essentially transcendental and otherworldly item such as (depending on one's clan) a concept, an idea, a sense (sinn), a proposition, or a thought.

It is a striking characteristic of Descartes that he brings thinking back to—*embeds* it in—nature. For him, thinking—*penser*—is essentially *penser-le-monde*, so well put in French, without a mediative preposition such as "about" or "of," an unabashedly direct object construction, thinking the world, exactly like kissing the gal, kicking the soccer ball and eating the ice cream. For Descartes, there is only Nature, the one and only. The kissing, the eating, and the thinking all take place in it, and a *place* they all take.

*This is a personal preface. If you can't stand those (I used to smirk at them), just skip it and go directly to chapter 1.

Descartes makes me, a reader, feel that this is how things *must* stand in the end. But at the outset, he also makes me feel—how *could* something like thinking ever occur *in* nature? This is the problem of the book.

This book is a sequel. Ten years ago, the project driving the earlier *What Am I?* came to all turn on one key *sentence* of Descartes', his response to a ticklish question by the ever-irrepressible Princess Elizabeth (to be found a letter written on 28 June 1643; CSM III). Descartes' response reads, in the original, "Et enfin, c'est en usant seulement de la vie et des conversations ordinaires, et en s'abstenant de méditer et d'étudier aux choses qui exercent l'imagination, qu'on apprend à concevoir l'union de l'âme et du corps." In my own free translation, "Finally, it is by relying on life and ordinary conversations, and by abstaining from meditating and studying things that exercise the imagination, that we learn how to conceive the union of mind and body."

I am still stuck with their exchange.

I still think the key to Descartes' way of placing man in nature lies in this admonition, in his wish to look at what he'd call in French *l'union vecu*—a pregnant phrase, with the verb connoting both "the union as *experienced*" and, more critically, "the union as *lived*." Ten years later, I hope to have a new key to Descartes' idea that coming to grips with (i) the thinking *by* men and (ii) their being essentially *thinking* men, rests on looking at how we live by thinking.

In teaching Descartes, I have accumulated many human debts. I owe specific thanks to Erin Eaker, Stavroula Glezakos, Erin Taylor, Keith Kaiser, Jorah Dannenberg, Sarah Coolidge, outstanding teachers, at UCLA, of Descartes and of the philosophy of mind. Coolidge improved much the final version of the typescript with sobering comments. The deepest debt among my students I owe to Dominik Sklenar, a most creative metaphysician, so creative that current professional philosophy alienated him to the point that he left it.

I struggle below, especially in chapters 5–6, with ideas of both Tyler Burge and John Carriero about the problems of knowledge and skepticism; both are colleagues from UCLA. I learned much by studying two of Burge's papers, one on Descartes and one on the notion of a priori knowledge, and I urge the reader, in the relevant chapters below, to have the papers before him. Carriero's forthcoming book on the Meditations, as well as co-teaching with him, have been an inspiration.

As will be obvious throughout this book, especially in chapters 2, 3, and 6, I owe a debt to Keith Donnellan for his notion of "having a thing in mind." (Donnellan's notion is a close cousin of Descartes' notion of the "objective reality" of an idea.) Here too, as with Burge, I did not fully appreciate, at the time, the richness of his ideas. It took me some time, and it was reflection on Descartes in the late 1990s, after Keith had retired, that made me see Donnellan's full depth.

Barbara Herman read my work and told me with her characteristic directness what she thought about it.

I have been sustained through the years by the friendship and comments of Lilli Alanen, Andrea Bianchi, David Chalmers, Steve Yablo, Michael Della Rocca, David Kaplan, Paul Hoffman, Sten Lindstrom, Paolo Leonardi, Tom Nagel, Mike Thau, Mohan Matthen, and Howie Wettstein. Special thanks to Moriel Zelikowsky, to Fabien and the Cafe Flore gang.

Of great help were the comments of the generous readers for Oxford University Press and the wise and always kind handling by the editor, Peter Ohlin, without whom . . .

I dedicate this book to two great teachers. The first is the mathematician Serge Lang, who just passed away this last September, the most natural teacher I ever met. The other is Keith Donnellan, whom I consider *my* teacher on matters of mind and metaphysics.

Acceglio, Valle Maira, Italy, July 2007

Contents

1. Synopsis: The Thinking-Man Paradox, 3

2. Thinking about the Sun I: The Fundamental Case, 21

3. Thinking about the Sun II: Thinking-about versus Knowing-which, 35

4. Thinking about God (and Nature-as-a-Whole), 47

5. Descartes' Cosmological Invariants I: Thinking, 63

6. Descartes' Cosmological Invariants II: Knowing, 75

Notes, 97

Index, 115

Cogito?

ONE

Synopsis: The Thinking-Man Paradox

The proposition in this book's title is Descartes'.[1] My contribution
is merely the addition of a question mark. The story behind the
question mark is the story of this book.

It is not the first time I have focused in writing on this one proposition, *Cogito*, or, in English, *I think*. For two decades, I have been
somewhat obsessively hunting the same white whale, what I will
call Descartes' *thinking-man paradox*. The puzzle is encapsulated in
the truth of this proposition. Goaded by Descartes, we are made to
wonder: How can there be *in* nature—as part and parcel *of* nature—
a human being, the one and only being in nature that *thinks*? *Cogito*,
the proposition declaring defiantly that such a fact obtains here and
now, is one of the oddest propositions I can think of. On the one
hand, it is promulgated by Descartes as the most immediate and
evident of all propositions (or of all *facts*; a distinction to which I
will return). On the other hand, it is not clear how it—or any other
of its kind, thinking-facts—could obtain at all, in this otherwise
thought-less cosmos. I am absolutely certain that *Cogito* is true but
cannot for the life of me see how it could be true of one of nature's
own products. Thus, Descartes' thinking-man paradox.

I hope the use of the loaded term "paradox" will not make me
appear to be one of those paradox-slingers. My latent tendency (in
my other life as a professional philosopher of language/logic) is
rather to lean in the other direction and to find no paradox where
the standard appellations agitate about Saul Kripke's paradox for
his point man Pierre in London or Gottlob Frege's paradox of
informative identities or the Banach–Tarski paradox of a poor

3

single little orange decomposed and soon recomposed to make up the sun. In all such cases, my feeling has always been that there is no paradox because we all intuitively know (our theories notwithstanding) what's going on—for example, why Pierre both believes that London is pretty and believes that it is not. The nerve Descartes touches is categorically different.

After reading the *Meditations* front to back a hundred times, *especially* after reading it so many times, we have no way of saying how there could be such a thing as a thinking-man *in* nature—(i) a thinking-being, just as much as the angels and God, and unlike flowers and dogs and brutes, but (ii) up to his neck (indeed, higher up, up to his brain) *in* nature, just like flowers and dogs and brutes and thus unlike angels and God. In fact, the *Meditations* gives the best argument I have seen—precisely because it is not reductionist—of why thinkings-occurring-in-nature should come out an oxymoron. And yet man thinks. And man thinks *essentially* (i) *in* and (ii) *about* nature (there is nowhere else to be and nothing else to think about).

Some years back, I wrote a little monograph on one aspect of this mysterious proposition (fact). I was then focused on the grammatical subject of the proposition, the I (that's doing the thinking). For Descartes first asserts—*Cogito*, I *think* (and the closely related) *Sum*, I *exist*. He then takes stock and asks "Fine, I am thinking and (thus) I am. But what am *I*? What is this *I* that is-and-thinks?" It is thus that *I* composed a book called *What Am I?* (henceforth *WAI*) focused on the fabric of this *I*.

The present book complements things by focusing on the *predicate* (verb) of the proposition *I think*—my (your, anybody's) *thinking*. How could there be, in this otherwise absolutely thought-deprived cosmos, acts-of-*thinking*? As one might say, mimicking Descartes: "Very well, I am thinking. But what is this activity, thinking (that I engage in)?"

This then is my quest—what thinking is and what it is for a being like me, no divine or angelic being but irreversibly a human being—to *be* thinking. It thus seems that the fact that we all assume is, for Descartes, the most evident of all facts about me (you, etc.)—*that I (you, etc.) think*—is on my reading the most difficult to explain: how could I (you, anybody) be *thinking?*

This all sounds "parochially" metaphysical, but for Descartes it was, as it should be, also a *scientific* question. Like all great thinkers then and (one romantically hopes) even today, he did not quite drive a wedge between the science of nature and *its* philosophy. As I read Descartes, he was the first modern *cognitive scientist*. He was surely a scientist to his bone marrow. Among his scientific investigations—on top of the structure of space and motion and liquid flow in water pipes and refraction laws in optics and the perihelion movement of Mercury—was the focus on that exoticum of nature: mankind. In particular, Descartes was fascinated, and fascinated as a *natural* scientist, with what he took to be so distinctive—and *essentially* distinctive—about Man, his *cognitive* life.

Unlike the false cleavages of our age—between the brain-minded who smirk at soul-analysis and the soul-analysts who scoff at the pharmacological—Descartes wanted to understand at once the hydraulics of the brain's pipes just as he wanted to understand Princess Elizabeth's melancholy; he wanted to diagram for us the pineal gland as if it were a cuckoo clock, and yet he devoted a book-long treatise to analyzing the basis of our most complex passions, like generosity and admiration. He did it all in a unificatory spirit, a true naturalist unbending about the finest details, be they the (first-person) phenomenology of a cognitive state or its underlying (objective) hydrodynamics. For me, though not for my students, majors in psychology and neuroscience and theoretical biology, who view him as an antiquated old fogey, Descartes (like Freud after him) is a model cognitive scientist, seeking for Man *integration without reduction*: Man is part and parcel of nature all right, but Man is like nothing else under the sun.

By now, it may seem that I am whipping up too much of an air of magic (recall my use of "paradox"), about thinking-acts-in-nature. Did not Descartes explain thinking-acts in nature by pointing back to the special fabric of the thinking subject (this sends us

back to the topic of my earlier book, *WAI)?* Did he not think that
I—the subject—have a mind, whose sole essence is to be: a thinking being?

The implicit suggestion here is that the puzzle regarding the
predicate "is thinking" (how it could apply in nature) is to be
defused by understanding better the *subject,* the one who is doing
the thinking. This classical reading of Descartes I called in *WAI
separatist dualism.* The picture dissolves the mystery—of what
I am—by creating a deeper one: I, the human being Joseph Almog,
am a composite-derivative entity, the ingredients of which are
two metaphysical primes. The one is nature-made, my body. The
other, my mind, is not. It is essentially nature-transcendent. Separatist dualism made it a sine qua non of my being in nature that
my mundane body be enlivened by a supernatural ingredient, my
mind. This last's transit in nature is a flash in the pan. Its existence
and essence—to be a thinking being—are totally independent
of the goings-on in nature. When nature takes its course and my
body turns to ashes and dust, my mind—the immortal unnatural
thing that it is—is destined to go back up to the heavens and per-
sist in its immaterial thought-ful existence.

Does this mind/body separatist dualism defuse the mysteries?
In my earlier book, I argued that it does not explain—from inside
Descartes' full set of naturalist-scientific concerns—what I am.

And twice over. First, it does not get right his full view of
the mind–body–man trio, of what I am. But, second, it also mis-
reads his general methodology. On my reading, Descartes never
separates for distinction's sake; he separates *ingredients* in order
to unify them better, in order to show us what pieces make up
the unified jigsaw puzzle. On the analogy of the common French
idiom *reculer pour mieux sauter* ("step back to jump better"), I read
Descartes as living by the maxim *separer pour mieux unifier* ("separate to unify better").[2]

On the specific mind–body–man front, I argued that whatever
are ultimately the three "unknowns"—man, mind, body—of this
Cartesian equation, for Descartes, *all* three must be nature-made,
nature-bound, and such that their individual nature, their essence,

is conferred on them *by* nature. I called this alternative form of dualism (for a duo of mind/body it still admits) *integrative dualism*. Its cornerstone is the primality of the full man Joseph, a man who is a substance/subject *of* nature. What is more, the man Joseph is a substance whose two *essential* ingredients—my *human* mind and body—are themselves each a fully intra cosmic substance, each *integral* to that cosmic kind of being, *man*kind. Both my mind and body are thus essentially not, for example, an angel's, but a *man's* mind and body.

Now, a few years later, I still think that integrative dualism gets Descartes better on this specific front—what I am. But does this suffice to explain how I manage to think? In the introduction to *WAI*, I confessed to being deeply dissatisfied with the very terms in which the mind/body problem is classically cast. The classical language sets up the question as one about the *number* of subjects (substances) or, for that matter, properties involved—are my mind and my body two subjects (properties) or one? As I said there, taken internally, *within* this "metaphysical language," Descartes' approach of differentiating the trio of human mind, body, and being seems quite right. But the problem here may be precisely this "metaphysical language," a procrustean bed. We are being forced to play the game of *counting* entities—how many substances are involved?—rather than *understanding* what it is for human beings to have emerged in cosmic history and be the distinct kind of thinking creatures they are.

In the last decade, reflecting on the incompleteness of the mind/body language of the earlier book, I have come to feel that if only I'd control better Descartes' thinking-man paradox—how there could be such things—I'd understand better what I am. The questions of how I, the ordinary man Joseph, am in a position to be thinking and how it became possible for anything at all to be thinking seem to me way more fundamental—and fundamental for Descartes—than the internal scholastic question of how many substances hide under my baseball cap. As I mentioned in the preface, I still think the key to an understanding of Descartes lies in his admonitions to Princess Elizabeth in his letter of 28 June 1643.

I simply have come to have a new understanding of what it means to look at the life of thinking-man, his living *by* thinking.[3]

What Is Thinking? Epistemological versus Metaphysical Questions

I speak of puzzlement about the very idea of thinking-man, as if the very idea is a contradiction in terms. But to many, my students included, my professed puzzlement on behalf of Descartes is itself mysterious. Does not Descartes himself elect, and with great theatrical drama, early in Meditation II, his own thinking—and its linguistic self reporting by means of *Cogito*—as the most *self-evident* fact of all, the *Archimedean point?* What could be so puzzling about the one fact that is the most primal of all, most self-evident of all, and the most immune to doubt of all?

Most of my students feel that, yet again, I am whipping up a feel of magical mystery, when things—what's on Descartes' mind—could not be clearer. Just as mind, as essentially thinking and distinct from body, is Descartes' solution to the problem of *who* is (and *what* does the) thinking, is not the fact of *my thinking*—my self-witnessed *Cogito*—his solution to the evil genius's all-out attack on our flimsy justifications for our common beliefs? The fact of my thinking is Descartes' new starting point for a re-founded—and this time around *well*-founded—system of justified beliefs. Does he not say loud and clear that this is his Archimedean point?

In laying out to the students what I take Descartes' thinking-man project to be, I call their attention to three seemingly separate issues—an obvious *textual* issue (in what *order* should we read the Meditations?), an *interpretive* question about "the Archimedean point" (what does Descartes *mean* by calling it thusly?), and, finally, a question about the very *purpose* of skeptical cases—what is he trying to accomplish by wheeling in the trio of maybe-I-am-dreaming, maybe-I-am-mad, and maybe-an-evil-demon-is-manipulating-me?

First, the textual issue. My question to the class is this: Are we to read Descartes' *Meditations* from I to II through to VI or are we to start at the end, with Meditation VI, and only when it has been drilled into our minds, go back to the beginning and read Meditations I, II, III, and so forth?

Descartes obviously starts his *Meditations* with Meditation I—who could doubt that?—and Meditation I culminates with the ubiquitous evil genius's skeptical argument, immediately followed, early in Meditation II, with my own thinking—my *Cogito*—as my elected *epistemological* response to the demon, the one absolutely justified axiom I can counter him with (here "axiom" means, of course, "as basic as one could get in the *justificatory* pecking order").

In contrast, *metaphysical* issues come only later. Questions such as What am I (the thinker)? What is the nature of thinking? How is thinking—as an activity—different in nature from imagining and visually perceiving and sensing pain? are all addressed later. Indeed, the full metaphysics of cognitive faculties—how the faculties arise in the full man, in his union of mind-and-body—are questions discussed only in the final Meditation, VI. And so there arises a textual—and in teaching the text a derivative *pedagogical*—issue: Are we to read the Meditations in their *chronological* order—from I to VI—and, in tow, move slowly from epistemological issues regarding thinking to metaphysical ones? Or are we rather to start with the metaphysics of thinking, focus on its intended true description of all-that-is-in-nature in Meditation VI, and view the early Meditations, in a new light, as *derived back* from the now primal Meditation VI?

My second and related issue is interpretive: what are we to make of Descartes' claim that *Cogito* is his elected *Archimedean point*? What does it mean to elect some fact (or thought or truth) as an Archimedean point or as an axiom?

My third and final question to the students concerns what they have been waiting for all this time: What is the *point* of the skeptical stories of Meditation I? It is commonplace to assume that skepticism is—perhaps a host of skepticisms are—making a splash appearance right in Meditation I because skepticism is of critical concern to Descartes: if our project is to re-found our *knowledge*, what could be more poignant than the display of the threat of skepticism, a coup de grâce to a naive yet alluring theory of *justification* of the beliefs we are all unreflectively wedded to?

Meditation I would then bring out how rotten the presupposed foundations are. The subsequent development from Meditations II to VI would then re-found our knowledge, only to end up with Meditation VI, presenting us with a now secure and well justified system (really, *architecture*) of knowledge, with the all-powerful skeptical virus finally contained. The kind of hypothetical meltdown of our justifications—displayed by the cases of Meditation I ("the virus")—has now been ruled out for good.

On the other hand, what are we to make of the *point* of skepticism, if we start with Meditation VI and an account of the *true nature* of thinking? Is there any point left to such tall tales? It is as if the skeptical virus has gone by the board; Meditation VI has no room for such fantasies. And, what is more, the hypothetical possibilities we are meant to worry about are, with VI deeply entrenched in us,... no *possibilities* at all. If so, what are the histrionics of Meditation I and early Meditation II all about?

When we are metaphysically oriented, one feels like saying (at least I do)—here as everywhere else, Joseph Butler's maxim applies, and everything, including every cognitive thing, is what it is and not another thing—dreaming is dreaming, madly hallucinating is madly hallucinating, and thinking is thinking; why mix apples and oranges? What in the world is Descartes *doing* with these cases? If we think of him purely in "political terms," that is, as raising the fear factor, why is a metaphysician bent on explaining how thinking *actually* works trying to scare us by weaving a tall story about a metaphysically impossible—indeed, as we will see, logically incoherent—evil genius?

Three questions. In laying out to the students a way to reconfigure our understanding of Descartes' project of thinking-man,

I start with the textual issue. It soon leads to observations regarding what I see him as meaning by "Archimedean point" and what the point of invoking skeptical cases is.

Starting with VI: Foundationalist versus Regressive Methodology

In describing Descartes' project of thinking-man, the central text I base myself on is Descartes' *Meditations*, with special emphasis on Meditations I, II, III, and VI. For some years, I followed the standard methodology (and the explicit order of the Meditations) and started with (to the students riveting) Meditation I and its seeming skeptical doubts, leading soon to Meditation II (and its ubiquitous *Cogito*, supposedly a safe haven from such skepticism); next, to Meditation III (What is it for me to think, to have an idea, of the sun? What is it to think, to have the idea, of God?); and then the grand finale, Meditation VI, where the dualisms (of mind and body and of thinker and nature-thought-of) are integrated. By week 8 of the class, as we read Meditation VI, we would try to *make up* a man out of a mind and body; in turn, we would try to *make up* a thinking act out of the already separately given (i) thinking mind and (ii) external nature. Through and through, I emphasized to the class that this methodology followed a particular "flow diagram" that I characterized, following Descartes, as *the analytic method*, or, using my own terms, the procession *from axioms to theorems*: Meditations I, II, and III lay conceptually fundamental principles, and Meditation VI derives from them subject-matter specific theorems (a direct feel for this approach may be given by Descartes' own presentation in his appendix to his second replies).

After fifteen years of following this sequence, I reversed my methodology of teaching. For the last decade, I have been starting the class with the last episode, Meditation VI. I explain to the class that here we get the structure of nature-as-a-whole, Descartes' final *cosmology*: what categories of things and activities there are and their essential interdependencies. In Descartes' own words in Meditation VI:6:[4]

> If nature is considered in its general aspect, then I understand by the term nothing other than God himself, or the ordered system of created things established by God.

Describing this ordered system consists of his writing down in Meditation VI, one by one, what I call in class Descartes' *nature-theorems*: the *specific* features and interdependencies of the constituents of the cosmological nexus, be they God, material kinds of things, mathematical kinds of things, the essential features of Man's mind-and-body union, the essential features of his cognitive life: what is thinking, what is dreaming, what it is to perceive pain, what it is to imagine a triangle, what is sensing, and so forth.

Having made a repertoire of the basic facts of nature and the natures of the involved constituents (what kind of thing each item is), I suggest to the class that we read the first few Meditations using what Descartes calls *the synthetic method* or, using my own terms, the method of *deriving axioms from theorems*—what underlying features ("axioms") nature must be endowed with to *explain* the variety of nature-theorems in Descartes' repertoire.

Borrowing a distinction (taken from Bertrand Russell) from the early twentieth-century philosophy of mathematics about the question "where do axioms come from?" I characterize the contrast between the two methodologies as between *foundationalist* axiomatics (and metaphysics) and *regressive* axiomatics (and metaphysics).

Doubtless, Descartes may be read as a foundationalist metaphysician, perhaps as the paradigm of the tradition. Surely, in institutional France, when something is described as "*cartésien*," they proudly think of the man as the icon of the method—from self-evident axioms (first principles) to theorems (specific applications). In truth, they are not so much concerned with specific foundationalist mathematical projects (as were Gottlob Frege and Ernst Zermelo) but with, so to speak, axioms for everything in life, from the curriculum of the Republic's elementary schools to the content of the entry exams for its *Grandes Écoles*, the plotting of the *Grands Boulevards* of Paris, and all the way to the architecture of pharaonic airports, museums, and libraries. Indeed, *architecture* is the key word, and *cartésien* is the best compliment that could be given to it—a few simple clear notions grounding very complex edifices.[5]

Descartes may be read as a reconstructionist foundationalist, a *"cartésien."* But I read Descartes like other great scientists-mathematicians who urged systematization of existing practiced mathematics at the turn of the twentieth century, such as Leopold Kronecker (and his co-author Heinrich Weber) and Georg Cantor and Richard Dedekind, and David Hilbert. They each wrote a volume called (something like) *The Foundations of . . . ,* and so may superficially seem to be engaged in a Frege-like foundationalism. They stipulated therein that they start with a clean, immaculate first page (as if they were on the first day of Genesis with barely light upon the water). But, in fact, unlike Frege, they were on the seventh day, with the immensely rich variety of the phenomena of mathematical practice—ideal numbers and zeta functions and cyclotomic fields and Riemann surfaces, and so forth—already engendered and interlaced and laid out before them, inviting them to provide descriptively adequate regressive axiomatizations. The same can be said for Descartes. There is a foundationalist-sounding rhetoric of restarting everything from square one. In fact, Descartes has in front of him the riches of practiced mathematics, from Pappus to Apollonius and all the way to Archimedes.[6]

The regressive scientist in him does not merely make a regressive mathematician; he is simply a regressive *thinker par excellence.* The task is always to deliver *back,* in one's system, what has been recognized beforehand as a truth of nature. Descartes first immerses himself in the full cosmology of the universe around him, taking inventory in his naturalist's diary of the variety of nature's theorems. When he writes them down, one by one, he recognizes the more and more unexpected ones—*dirt exists* (Marin Mersenne's example, to which Descartes responds) is surprising but not as surprising as *flies exist*; in turn, *flies exist* is surprising but not as surprising as *dogs exist*; *dogs exist* is surprising but not as surprising as *men exist*; and of the many activities engaged by this last creature—*Respiro, Ambulo, Percipio,* and so forth—none exceeds in subtlety *Cogito*. Even if the *reports* in the first-person voice *Respiro, Ambulo, Percipio,* and so forth cannot be produced by my dog Jig, they are *true* of it—Jig does breathe, walk, and perceive. There is no way, there absolutely *cannot* be a way, in the strictest sense of possibility and essence, for *Cogito* to be true of Jig.

The Hunt for an Archimedean Point

Since 1641, when Descartes wrote, there have been a myriad of attempts to read his hunt for an "Archimedean point" in an *epistemological* way, searching for this one inner *thought* that is as self-evident, by which I mean as evident-to-the-self, and as resistant to the machinations of the evil genius as could be. It is thus that the *Cogito* has been anointed as the most intimate, most subjectively inalienable and trustworthy thought. The subject here searches inside himself for a thought that is *not* revelatory of the world but that, to the contrary, is independent of it and would hold no matter (i) what the world is like and (ii) whether there is any world at all to think of. As my students are fond of saying (and they are here in agreement with a procession of eminent analytic and continental metaphysicians), "Even if there were no world, my *Cogito* would still shine through. ..." When the search is oriented this way, I see us as hunting for what I will call an *epistemological Archimedean point*.

This was not what Archimedes meant by an Archimedean point. According to my encyclopedia, he rather meant

> a vantage point from which an observer can objectively perceive the subject of inquiry, with a view of totality. The ideal here is of "removing oneself" from the object of study so that one can see it in relation to all other things.

I read Descartes as searching for an Archimedean point in Archimedes' sense (and, as one learns to expect from Descartes, with a more ambitious twist: whereas Archimedes promised to lift the whole earth once placed in such a standpoint, Descartes was looking to "lift" the whole universe, the cosmos, from such a point). On my reading, Descartes was looking for a fact that is as structurally revelatory about the nature of the world as a whole (the wondering subject included) as any fact could be. If, in trying to understand the world, we could only keep reminding ourselves, "But remember, this is a world that is as subtle as giving rise to *Cogitos*—to men thinking!" we'd go a long way toward understanding the nature of the rest of the cosmos. When the hunt is oriented this way, I will call it a quest for a *cosmological Archimedean point*.

A Basic Corollary: The Illusory Character of Skepticism

And now, finally (!), to what is on every student's mind, our third question—what is the point of the skeptical cases of Meditation I? If Descartes' project is not one of prescriptive epistemology, if it is indeed a descriptive project of unraveling (stacks of) cosmological structure, what are the dramatic scenarios meant to achieve?

Reading Meditation I, my students are quite confident that its point is to *argue* that the very same objectual-thinking I am now having—for example, to follow Descartes, I will suppose I am thinking of the sun—could be taking place even if (i) it was not the sun but an object looking like it, a twin, that was causing my thinking episode, (ii) if I were dreaming, (iii) if I were mad (e.g., hallucinating a sunlike object without one in nature), (iv) if there were an evil genius who fabricated all my thinkings but with no outside nature whatsoever. My question in response to these strong independence feelings is: What is the origin of the idea that the *success* in thinking is (i) automatic and (ii) guaranteed throughout all these background conditions?

The Internal/External Distinction

My conjecture (to be turned below into a thesis) is this: something as simple as it is attractive in our account of thinking makes it *seem* possible that thinking (specifically, of the sun) is literally "automatic" and independent of the specific cosmic facts we happen to be surrounded by. We cherish a distinction—often regarded as originally "Cartesian"—between an *internal* space (our mind, thought of as a box of some sort) and an external *space*, often called, as if the appellation is absolutely innocent, *the external world* (thus presupposing there is a correlate "internal world"). We see the internal space as consisting of *cognitive media* for which we have a variety of theoretical titles—"ideas," "concepts," "representational contents"—by virtue of which, and *only* by virtue of which, our mind reaches out and gets to the external things and the ways they are.[7]

Given this internal space of cognitive media, it is most natural to believe that they exist independently of any cosmic conditions—and as we will see, modern views calling themselves "externalist" hold on to this temptation regarding *existence,* even if they cunningly *index* the identity ("individuation") of these media. The very feasibility of applying *given* thoughts to a spectrum of alternative universes had seemed to depend on the fact that the thought-ingredients, our ideas, are given *prior* to and *independently* of any particular universe and are thus applicable to them all (all possible or conceivable/imaginable universes).

Descartes' own early remarks in Meditation I on our dreaming (thinking, imagining, hallucinating) of chimeras and sirens had been read as stating this much: If our dreaming (imagining, thinking, etc.) of sirens depended on the actual existence of sirens, we would not succeed in doing so. We do succeed. So the pertinent cognitive medium "representing" sirens must be given prior to and independently of the real cosmos.

Some would insist in response (and Descartes' own initial move in Meditation I seems of the kind) that as siren-independent as our siren-thinking is, perhaps it is not independent of *everything* there actually is (for we do make the images of sirens and chimeras out of encounters with real animals and female faces). Perhaps so. But still two points would seem to be made by the skeptic: (i) our chimeras- and sirens-thinking is successful independently of there being sirens and chimeras, and (ii) by parity of form, must not our thinking of horses and real women be as independent of the real existence of such items?

The point simmering here is not merely *epistemological*: how can I *know* that my thinking of horses is not as horses-free as my thinking of sirens is sirens-free? The key claim the skeptic (or at least my preferred skeptic) is after is a *metaphysical* thesis about what is necessary for a certain kind of thinking to come to be (never mind whether we know it did): if sirens-thinking can take place without sirens, horses-thinking can take place without horses.

This seeming metaphysical independence is, in my view, enough for the skeptic to put his foot in the door. Of course, he will need to work more on putting the other foot in—how far can we *generalize* beyond sirens and chimeras, women and horses—and argue that such a vivid contemplation, a full life of the mind, may be going on without the corresponding elements of nature? Can we really subtract the whole of nature (perhaps with only a diaphanous evil genius on hand) and still make sense of a rich arsenal of thinkings going on?

So the skeptic needs to develop his case. But suppose we can vindicate the underlying classical *mediative* theory of the cognitive bond driving the skeptic. This rests on the contrast between a pre-nature *internal* space of independently existing cognitive media (e.g., my idea[s] of the sun or of sirens) and a post-thinking *external* world of things (e.g., the sun proper and no sirens). We merely *apply* to nature the already grasped ideas—to find out their "referents"—and the thoughts thought—to find out their truth values. And now skepticism looms: the very same ideas and thoughts might well be had "in my mind" (in the internal space), even if nature (the external realm) was very different or had altogether washed away.

On the other hand, suppose we show, as I believe Descartes aimed in Meditation III, that the mechanism of thinking (for him, of having *ideas*, of what it means to *have* the sun in my mind) runs in quite the opposite way. It is essentially nature-dependent, with the sun as its source and activator. What is more, there is nothing automatic about it—the window of opportunity for successful thinking, of *succeeding* in having the sun in my mind, is very narrow. Stronger yet, suppose that we question, as I believe Meditation III and the first replies to Caterus demand us to, the very language of internal/external worlds. There is only one receptacle, the all-embracing nature, and both the sun and my thinking-of-it are part of it. If you will, both are *internal* to this receptacle (there is nowhere else to be). Or, if you will, both the sun and my thinking of it are in the *external* world (again, there is nowhere else to be).

Or better yet, we should not use the internal/external language at all. We should simply say how exactly one cosmic event, really an *act*, my thinking of the sun, depends on another event, the sun's existence. If we follow Descartes' bread crumbs on this last question, as given in Meditation III and especially the first and fourth replies, I believe the possibility—stronger yet, the very coherence—of skepticism will be exposed as illusory.

Once Again: The Thinking-Man Paradox

As I see things, for Descartes the thinking-man paradox all hangs on this one fact: the cosmos has in it that kind of thing, thinking man. This, for Descartes, is absolutely fundamental, a true Archimedean point. And yet it is a most perplexing fact (anything but *self-evident*): it is as fundamental a fact about nature as could be, and it is as fundamental a fact—*Cogito*—about each of us as could be. Nonetheless, it is not clear how something engendered *by* nature—just like *its* dirt and flowers and cats—could be doing this seemingly *un*natural thing, thinking.

The breaking up, in a man's stomach, of the molecules making up the breakfast brioche, the detecting of photons by his retina, the processing of serotonin in his neurons, are all part of nature taking *its* course; but . . . thinking? Is does seem at first blush an act *against* nature. But how could this be, the Archimedean point of nature turning out *un*natural? There must be something falsely antagonistic in our understanding of both nature and thinking. We must start afresh.

TWO

Thinking about the Sun I:
The Fundamental Case

In this chapter I am focused on one (kind of) thinking fact—my thinking of the sun. By way of preamble, let us keep in mind two "technical" features of the discussion that follows.

Two Preambles

First, the choice of this object of thinking, the sun. Descartes discusses, in Meditation III and in various replies, other objects-of-thinking: God, infinity (to objectify: infinite substance), angels, complex machines, triangles, material bodies, my-self (that is, his self), all cases with more philosophical bite than this mundane object, the sun. I believe however that if we clear up some elementary facts in this mundane case (where the extra bite doesn't intrude), we will have the essentials of Descartes' account of thinking of objects, whatever their fabric. So, not to worry, we will soon get to thinking of God and oneself. But hard cases make bad law. In contrast, mundane cases make a pretty good law; indeed, so good, in Descartes' clever hands, that the law survives the hard cases.

Second, the order of discussion I follow is different from the usual one in yet another way. Discussions of the fact of my thinking—or even of (any) man's thinking—proceed often first at the general level, by comparing thinking-in-general (sometimes "intellection") to other faculties—perception, imagination, and so forth. Then, and quite separately, we broach a seemingly less central question—raised only in Meditation III and the first replies—of what it is to think of *specific things*; for example, think of the sun or of triangles or of (nonexistent) sirens and chimeras. We discuss thinking-of-specific-things as *derivative* and *posterior to* thinking-in-general.

I suggest that we proceed in the opposite fashion. We first need to understand what Descartes says about *specific thinkings*—my thinking of the sun, God, bodies, triangles, myself, and so forth. In explaining these cases, he explains the critical notion of my having nature's things, and nature itself, *in* my mind, and thus of me thinking-the-world (in French, *penser le monde*, without the preposition, conveys the idea well).

Thinking about the Sun: Five Principles

What does Descartes say about my thinking of the sun?

His account can be summarized in five fundamental principles, to be laid out in the current chapter and the next one. The four last principles are genuinely theoretical *principles*. The first is rather a quasi-empirical *observation* about how we *actually* operate as cognitive beings. This observation is essentially negative. Descartes presents data against a cluster of theories of thinking—what was called in chapter 1 the *mediative-content* approach.

First Principle: The Inadequacy of Predicative Contents

Descartes' first observation is intended to argue against a presupposition that had become common before his time (and way after; e.g., in Frege's theory of thought), that thinking of the sun works by resemblance between *internal* representors and *external* objects. Put more "technically," we seek to match (i) predicative contents held in ("grasped by") our minds with (ii) worldly objects—such as the sun. The predicative contents are meant to be the information we'd provide if asked "Which thing is the sun?"—the information with which our mind searches the external world to identify the sun. Descartes mentions two such predicative "ideas," one phenomenal, one theoretical. The passage here occurs early in Meditation III:[1]

> And finally, even if these ideas did come from things other than myself, it would not follow that they must resemble those things. Indeed, I think I have often discovered a great disparity <between an object and its idea> in many cases. For example, there are two different ideas of the sun which I find within me. One of them, which is acquired as it were from the senses and which is a prime example of an idea which I reckon to come from an external source, makes the sun appear very small. The other idea is based on astronomical reasoning, that is, it is derived from certain notions which are innate in me (or else it is constructed by me in some other way), and this idea shows the sun to be several times larger than the earth. Obviously both these sides cannot resemble the sun which exists outside me; and reason persuades me that the idea which seems to have emanated most directly from the sun itself has in fact no resemblance to it at all.

This is a natural "negative" argument that was to be repeated and amplified three centuries years later—without conscious knowledge that something ancient is being replayed—against the paradigm (modern) thinking-by-content theory, Frege's analysis of the act of thinking and what is being thereby thought. It would not surprise me to find it—the negative argument—in the writings of philosophers operating two millennia before Descartes (around 350 BC) or in medieval times. It is bound to come up time and again once the dominant paradigm theory of thinking is a thinking-by-mediative-content model.

TWO MEDIATIVE PREDICATIVE MODELS

When I speak of thinking-of-the-sun by means of intermediaries, I would like to distinguish two historically significant models. The famous articulation of one model is modern, primarily by Frege and Russell. I will call it the *representational content* (RC) *model.* The other model's most well known articulation is found in Aristotle and Aquinas, and I will call it the *matter-form* (MF) *model.*[2]

In the RC model, we keep the *ontology* of the ultimate objects, for example, the sun, mundane. The sun, as an object, is just that—the sun—with no extra logical-conceptual decompositions. The mediative content shows in the mechanism linking the thinker and the target object. It thus shows not in the ontology of objects proper but in the ontology of cognitive relations (and the associated epistemology—how thinkers know objects). The thinker primarily grasps a representational content (a Fregean *sinn* or some other such representational predicative information); it is this predicative content—for example, *largest object in the solar system* or *big orange like object sinking into the sea at sunset*—that is being thought of primarily. This content, in turn, *denotes* (is satisfied by) some in-nature object, in our case the star known as the sun. It is in virtue of these two relations that I, the thinker, can derivatively think about the denotation, the sun. There is no way—and "no" here is a logical "no" pertaining to the very *type* of relation involved—for me to think of the sun without such a denoting content.

In the MF model, we design the *ontology* of the target objects so as to have in each such target an element (to some: a part)—the object's *form*—that is key to our thinking of it. Here the very metaphysics of the object contains a mind-receptive element. Thinking of the object is conditional upon "receiving" its form. Paul Hoffman puts it well: if anything is direct in our thinking, it is direct thinking of *forms*; in virtue of apprehending directly the form, we think derivatively of the object whose form it is, an object which *is* (constituted by) by this distinct matter-form combination.[3]

I am sure that for many purposes the difference between the two models is fundamental. But not for the point I am about to illustrate in Descartes' thinking. For on both models, it is the apprehension of basic predicative information (be that information encoded in the object's form or in the way of being given [*sinn*] the object) that forges the thinking of the in-nature object.

I think of the sun because and *only* because I employ the *predicative telescope* (be it the form or the *sinn*) to the object. The hold of the mind on an object is never direct; it is mediated by the telescoping predicate(s) *making* the object intelligible to the mind. On both models, there is no thinking of an object without predicative representation, without predicative *denotation*, of the object.

THE REFUTATION OF THE PREDICATIVE
TELESCOPE MODEL

I will focus in what follows on the RC variant of the predicative telescope methodology for two reasons. First, among uses of the predicative telescope to account for thinking-about, I understand this variant better than others. Second, when we are after a comparison of Descartes' refutation of the predicative telescope mechanism with recent modern refutations, it is the RC model (in its Frege–Russell version) that is most ubiquitous.

I said earlier that in each period, when the model of thinking by an intermediate predicative telescope becomes the paradigm mechanism, refutations naturally pop up. And indeed, in our times, with the Frege–Russell form of the RC model reining the theory of thinking about, negative arguments started emerging in the middle of the twentieth century. The purest form of this negative argument was given in the mid-1960s by Keith Donnellan and, a bit later, in other, more mixed forms, by David Kaplan, Saul Kripke, and Hillary Putnam. In effect, in our time, we have a cluster of arguments against the treatment of the predicative content as the mechanism of having-in-mind. Of the many such variant negative arguments across history I am familiar with, I find Descartes' argument to be the purest and the strongest. So, far from reading our contemporary arguments back into Descartes,' I find his to be the paradigm argument. Let me explain this.[4]

Before I articulate the argument inherent in the sun passage, we need a terminological clarification. Descartes shifts between his use of "idea" here and in his main theoretical work, work we will analyze in stating his second principle (what I call *the one object, two modes of being* principle). In the sun passage just quoted, we find a mix of uses of "idea"—there is (i) the *causal*-process notion regarding what the idea is *of* (it is of the sun). But there is also reference to (ii) the *predicative content*, as if different predicative contents are *enough* to make it that we have two ideas in mind. Which is the leading use?

My solution is not to use the multiply ambiguous term "idea" in what follows. I will use "predicative profile" to describe the conglomerate of predicates I may offer when asked "So, JA, which thing is the sun?" And I will continue to speak of thinking-acts (or havings in mind), rather than of ideas, when I speak of the actual cognitive fact to be accounted for: my thinking of the sun.

Consider some object at the other end of the galaxy—a dark object *from* which Descartes himself never got information ("energy"). Let us call it *De-Sun*. And let us suppose De-Sun did strictly satisfy Descartes' scientific theory of the heavens. So De-Sun is the satisfier of Descartes' predicative profile; the profile *denotes* it. Should we say then that Descartes was thinking all his life about De-Sun because De-Sun matched better (indeed, uniquely!) his theory?

Surely not. Descartes was thinking of the one and only sun of ours, the only star in our planetary system. The two profiles he mentions are *of* the sun because they were generated by the sun. It was efficient causal interaction with the sun that led him at one point to form the predicative profile "Large shining orange ball"; it was again interaction with the sun that led him to come up with a theory describing "A massive object around which orbit the six(!) planets. . . ." Both predicates are false of the sun but both are profiles of the sun, not of other object(s) of which they are (may be), strictly speaking, true.[5]

Second Principle: One Object, Two Modes of Being

With Descartes' second principle, we are about to broach his own positive account of thinking (of the sun).

In Meditation III and in the first and fourth replies, Descartes uses at least two intuitive enough, vernacular-bound terminologies to describe the thinking-fact to be accounted for. Sometimes he speaks of *my thinking of the sun.* So here the focus is on thinking-facts, facts of the form *x thinks of y.* I will call this the *active form,* focusing as it does on my active role as the subject of the activity—thinking. In the first replies (picking up on Caterus's language) he speaks now in a *passive* form, as it were, with subject and object inverted, of *the sun's being conceived by me.* I will characterize this approach to the target fact as the *passive form.* He has now demoted me from the prime spot and given it to the sun. The sun is the focal point and Descartes is interested in its being-thought-of-by-me.

These are the two intuitive forms Descartes uses (in language) to get at the target thinking-fact. But there is a third form he uses in Meditation III (as in Meditations V and VI). It provides the formulation that attracts most of the philosophical press: *my having an idea of the sun* (in my mind). This formulation seems to mention a third intermediate item, on top of me and the sun, my *idea* of the sun. We seem to encounter here a sort of medium and go-between me and the sun, and many just go on and read Descartes to mean something of the following sort: *There exists a certain third thing, an idea of the sun, and I (the first thing) think of the sun (the second thing), in virtue of (by having, by apprehending, etc.) that intermediate thing.* Some go on to add, *and I think of the sun only in virtue of (only by having, etc.) that intermediate thing.* Not so, says Descartes in a most interesting gloss to Caterus:[6]

For example, if anyone asks what happens to the sun through its being objectively in my intellect, the best answer is that nothing happens to it beyond the application of an extraneous label which does indeed "determine an act of the intellect by means of an object." But if the question is about what the *idea* of the sun is, and we answer that it is the thing which is thought of, in so far as it has objective being in the intellect, no one will take this to be the sun itself with this extraneous label applied to it. "Objective being in the intellect" will not here mean "the determination of an act of the intellect by means of an object," but will signify the object's being in the intellect in the way in which its objects are normally there. By this I mean that the idea of the sun is the sun itself existing in the intellect—not formally existing, of course, as it does in the heavens, but objectively existing, that is, in the way in which objects normally are in the intellect. Now this mode of being is, of course, much less perfect than that possessed by things which exist outside the intellect; but, as I did explain, it is not therefore simply nothing.

This is still rather theoretical. But I will launch my account of Descartes' thinking-mechanism, the mechanism of having something in mind, from this basic passage. I call it the *one object, two modes of being* passage, to contrast (i) the claim made here of two modes of being of the sun (in the heavens vs. in my mind) but only one object, the sun, with (ii) the more common reading of *my having an idea of the sun*, where we identify only one mode of being—being *simpliciter*—but *two* objects, the sun-of-the-heavens and the sun-idea.

Let us call the sun's being in the heavens its *primary* mode of being and its being in a given (e.g. my) mind, its *secondary* mode of being. And so, we can say for Descartes: for me to be thinking of the sun, the sun must come to have, on top of its primary mode of being, this secondary kind of being (and specifically, in Almog's mind). It did have the primary mode for a few billion years and only recently came to have the secondary mode.

To bring out this *one object, two modes of being* approach of Descartes, I will use a notation reflecting his second formulation—in his response to Caterus—where he shifts to the passive voice by inverting object (the sun) and subject (JA), telling Caterus that my conceiving (thinking) of the sun is the sun's being conceived (thought) of by me. So on my notation for the structure of such thinking (having-in-mind) facts, the fact of *my (JA's)* thinking of the sun will be denoted by $Sun/thinking_{JA}$; the fact of Bill Clinton's thinking of the sun will be given as $Sun/thinking_{BC}$; and the generic (unspecified subject) fact of (some) thinking of the sun will be given as $Sun/thinking_{x}$.[7]

Third Principle: To Be Conceived
It Must Be Caused

So much for the *structure* of the thinking fact. Next, we ask: how did it come about? What *made* me have the sun (rather than, say, the moon) in mind?

Descartes' discussion often fuses two different questions I would like to separate. The first we may call the *preservation of reality* question, the second the *mechanism of having in mind* question.

The principle of preservation of reality concerns the notion of *grade* of reality (sometimes "perfection"): the effect cannot have more reality than the cause. Applied to ideas (that is, when the effect-event is a thinking-event, e.g., the effect is my thinking of the sun), we are told the effect cannot have more reality than its cause, in this case—the event of the sun's being in the heavens. This much concerns the transmission of reality grades by causal processes.

The second principle Descartes invokes is quite independent of the notion of grade-of-reality (let alone the objective/formal reality distinction for ideas). It concerns the *mechanism* by which the sun can *come* to have that secondary mode of being: be in my mind. Descartes is set here to hit two birds with one stone: (i) outlaw one type of mechanism, the *content-resemblance* mechanism and (ii) urge upon us a different mechanism, the (content-free) *by efficient causation* mechanism. Our focus in what follows brackets off matters of reality-preservation; we are exclusively concerned with the having-in-mind generation mechanism question.

In explaining my coming to think of the sun, Descartes' suggested "flow diagram" reverses the direction embraced by the meditative content models. We do not start inside my mind, in the "internal world" (wherever that is) and check my associated content only subsequently, to "look for" the sun, in "the external world," using the content-telescope ("which thing matches the predicative content?"). In line with our object/subject inverted notation, we *start* with the heavenly sun. The sun transmits, *in* nature, in the very medium of efficient causation, energy (light particles) that heats rocks, photosynthesizes plants, tickles the fur of cats, tans the skins of men, and hits the brains of thinkers. At this point, the thinking man—but not a sheer "brute" (Descartes' brand of Zombie) who only has the photons run from his retina to his brain and stop there—is ready to have the sun in his mind. For to have the sun in one's mind is not to have that huge fireball inside some internal space—mind space—in the sense that a tennis ball is lodged *in* my pocket. For one thing, immaterial minds notwithstanding, to have the sun in my *brain* is also not to have that huge ball of fire lodged in the very restricted space making up my physical brain.

Having *in* my mind (and earlier yet, having *in* my brain) is to be understood quite differently, or else we'd be confusing the secondary mode of being with the primary mode. We would be claiming incoherently that the sun exists in two spatial locations at the same time. To be in my mind (or for that matter, in my brain) is for the sun to be *related* just by this efficient causation process, a process transmitting from the sun information to my brain and mind. The sun impacts the rocks and the plants and the cats. But it also impacts human brains and thus, and only thus, the interlocked human minds. Each of the foregoing things—rock, plant, cat, man—are en-lightened targets—they all have the one and only sun in them. The differences lies rather in *how* these sun-processors come to *have* it, especially on the last leg from the sun—as we hit the surface of the rock or the depths of a mind. Of course, photosynthesis is one *way* of having the sun (in a flower); tanned skin is another *way* of having the sun (in my body). Finally, forming a visual image of the sun is a *way* for my mind (via my processing brain) to have the sun in it. There are other—nonimagistic—*ways* for my human mind to have the sun; one way, as in an example suggested by Descartes in *The World* (CSM I, 181), is by processing the *phrase (le) soleil*. But no matter how different the ways of having the sun, across kinds of being or inside a given individual, we must keep in mind the following two points:

(a) all of these *ways* involve efficient causation processes that are essentially sun-initiated.

(b) no matter what differences we spot in the processes-of-coming-to-have-it, these differences are in the *ways of* having it, not in the it-had or the intra nature causal basis of the process.

THE PAINTING PASSAGE

Descartes himself makes related very fine distinctions about the *origin* of ideas (of havings in mind) as impinging on the *identity* of the idea (having in mind):

> To provide a solution to your objection about the idea of God, we must observe that the point at issue is not the essence of the idea, in respect of which it is only a mode existing in the human mind and therefore no more perfect than a human being, but its objective perfection, which the principles of metaphysics teach must be contained formally or eminently in its cause. Suppose someone said that anyone can paint pictures as well as Apelles, because they consist only of patterns of paint and anyone can make all kinds of patterns with paint. To such suggestion we should have to reply that when we are talking about Apelles' pictures we are not considering just a pattern of colours, but a pattern skillfully made to produce a representation resembling reality, such as can be produced only by those very practiced in this art.

Descartes insists here on two distinctions. There is, first, the argument against individuation by matching looks. Thus, if we have two look-indiscernible "images" (be they photographs or paintings or "internal images") of, say, the sun and a twin sun,

Descartes will class them as two distinct ideas (idea-types), if they arise, as ours do, from different efficient causes. Second, fix now the originating object, say our sun. Consider now two qualitatively indiscernible sun-imagistic presentations, one accomplished by a painter, one by an automatic photograph. Descartes indicates he will take them to be two different ideas (idea-types).[8]

THE *TO BE IT MUST BE CAUSED* PASSAGE

Descartes insists on a causal activator of the thinking-of-the-sun fact, that is, of the sun's-being-in-my-mind fact. We may call this Descartes' *no mentation without inculcation* principle:[9]

(D) No being for a thing in my mind without a causal process inculcating information from *it* into my mind.

Descartes is quite explicit about (D) in Meditation III proper (CSM II, 28–29 top). But just in case the audience is offering to interpret him differently, as Caterus indeed does, he reiterates the point with added verve in his first replies. For in the first replies, Caterus proposes to Descartes to say about thinking of the sun (and eventually, of God), what he (Caterus) *took* Descartes himself to be saying in Meditation V about thinking-of-*triangles* (or of having the idea of triangles)—this thinking (having an idea) needs no cause. All the thinker needs to do is apprehend a trans-cosmic "true and immutable nature" (essence) and voila! he is successfully thinking of—triangles, God, the sun, and so forth. On Caterus's model, all of these essence-contemplations involve no *intra*cosmic causal commerce between the thinker and the external (spatiotemporal) world.[10]

In his response, in the first replies, Descartes is correcting Caterus twice over. First, the sun (and almost all such mundane objects) are not (more delicately: do not *have*) true and immutable natures. But second, even if they were—even if what enters the object position of the thinking-relation fact has (or, is identical with) an immutable fabric, this still does not explain why and how the item—immutable and eternal as it is—*became* the object of my thinking. *What* (immutable and trans cosmic) nature the object has is one issue; *how* I, intra cosmic as I am, came to think of the object is quite a different question. Even for the non concrete likes of God, triangles, and so forth, we need to explain what process *made* them *be* in my mind. And this explanation—of the *how come?*—always consists for Descartes of an intra cosmic generative efficient causal mechanism. He says:[11]

> But my shrewd critic sees all this quite well, and he therefore concedes that we can ask why a given idea contains such and such objective reality. His answer is that, in the case of all ideas, what I wrote in connection with the idea of a triangle holds good, namely that "even if perhaps a triangle does not exist anywhere, it still has a determinate nature or essence or form which is immutable and eternal." And this, he says, does not require a cause. But he is well aware that this is not an adequate reply; for even if the nature of the triangle is immutable and eternal, it is still no less appropriate to ask why there is an idea of it within us.

The passage presents us with Descartes' third principle, the *to be conceived it must be caused* principle. It describes the *existence condition* for a thinking act (equivalently: for having-in-mind—an-object): no having in mind of *x* without a generative process infusing a trace of *x* into my mind. In a word, in Descartes' word, we reencounter in the *to be conceived it must be caused* principle, the *no mentation without inculcation* principle (D) formulated earlier. The following chapter is dedicated to further reflection about this principle and its consequences.

THREE

Thinking about the Sun II: Thinking-about versus Knowing-which

This chapter continues our discussion of one kind of thinking fact, my thinking of the sun. The foregoing discussion culminated in Descartes' principle (D):

(D) No being for a thing in my mind without a causal process inculcating information from it into my mind.

The principle tends to engender two recurring worries in most students (audiences). Both concern the last segment in the sun-to-mind channel—the in-my-mind sun traces just mentioned. First, there is a worry about the *fabric* ("composition") of the sun-traces: what are the sun traces just mentioned made of? I will call this the *trace-fabric* question.

The second worry concerns the apparent dismissal of Descartes' *one object, two modes* principle. If we depend on a mind-*trace* of the sun for thinking of it, are we not back with a *two*-object "representational-content" theory? We seem to have a (i) *grasping* (deploying, processing, etc.) of the mind's sun-trace (. . . idea? image? etc.) and (ii) an "intentional"—content involving—relation between the trace and the sun, making the trace a trace-of-the-sun. Only when put together, (i) and (ii) induce (iii) my thinking of the sun. With (ii) admitted as indomitable, it seems we are now back with a meditative content account. Let me call this second objection the *representational-role* question.[1]

The Trace Fabric Question

The sun leaves traces in my brain, and, in turn, in my mind. Speaking now for Descartes, I do not say that the mind-traces are identical with (or even made of) matter-combinations. Indeed, I have not spoken about material composition, even when putting minds aside and attending to the presence of traces in physically based artifacts like photographs of the sun or words (names) naming it, such as the French *le soleil*. The fabric of the word *soleil* (or any other word) is not purely material; nor is a photograph (painting) of the sun given its identity by being reduced to identity with this or that material composition. Both the word and the photograph are "abstract" entities, at least in the sense that they are not *purely* material, not *identical* with a certain assembly of material particles. And what is good for the word and the photograph—they are not purely material—is good for the brain trace, the source of my mind trace of the sun.

Not purely material but not material-*free* either. None of these information-traces would have existed without a material basis. None would have existed without being causally generated by the specific material channel from which they actually were induced (on which *generation*, we enlarge in our fifth and last principle). So, though not *purely* material, these information-traces, whether in the brain or the mind, do *depend* for their existence on the material world (and specifically in the last leg, certain molecular alignments) while not being *identical* to material things (stuff).

So much—strict dependence but no reducibility (or identity)—I already argued, on behalf of Descartes, in *WAI*, as obtaining between the human mind and the human body (brain). In turn, the havings-in-mind of this mind—JA's mind, in short JAM—also depend in the strictest essentialist sense on the material cosmos, and in particular on the human being and the brain *of* whom this is the induced mind. There would be no sun-having in JAM, without JA, the human being; and this last would not exist without JA's body and brain (on the *WAI* reading of Descartes, JA's brain is essential to JA's body's existence and vice versa).

What makes each such materially based but abstract information-trace what it is, and is *distinctly*, is the efficient causal generative process by which it came to be—from the sun, by way of the material cosmos, and onto me (and my brain and mind) and onto my having the sun in *them* (in my brain, and *consequently*, in my mind).[2]

The Representational Role Question

Our second question is: should we think of this mind-having-the-sun as a new *object* or as a mere *way* of being of the sun? My answer on behalf of Descartes is independent of the fabric of the purported object, the trace. The question is as it were logical-conceptual, not material. This calls for some elucidation.

Various objects need to be cited to account for the way the sun came to be in . . . my *eye*. Further into my body, we find the retina, the intercranial "fiber optics," the neurons, and so forth, and last but not least, induced by this long procession, my mental image of the sun (a similar tale applies to the procession initiated at the sun and terminating in my mind's having the word *soleil*). All in all, the information channel from sun to mind is filled with—and is dependent on—a large plurality-procession of objects.

As I read Descartes, the question before us is not one of *facts*— are certain objects, such as photons or neurons or images, essentially involved in the information channel from sun to mind? For the factual answer—such and such items *are* involved—is agreed upon by all.[3] The question is rather of *theoretical organization*: what elements of the chain from sun to mind are merely *instrumental means*, and what, in contrast, is (are) the *essential* factor(s)— what I will call *the cognitive elixir*—without which there can be no thinking of what we like to call "the external world." It is in attempting this cut that we confront yet again (recall our early encounter in chapter 1) the influential readings (ex post facto as it were) of Descartes as a "representationalist," as if Descartes were a precursor of Kant and Frege and all the way to such leading contemporary "neo-Kantians (and Fregeans)," like David Kaplan and Tyler Burge.[4]

In my view (and mainly, to my *ear*), the language of current philosophy of mind is driven by a deep-seated "representationalism," as if the doctrine were both inevitable and self-evident. In turn, the claim *no mentation without representation* is viewed as axiomatic.

Three questions arise at this juncture. First, what on earth does this mean—what is this (crypto) representationalism we moderns all seem to view as inevitable? Second, is Descartes such a (crypto) representationalist? Third and finally, is representationalism indeed true?

I will here deal only with the first two questions. I will make a special effort to put away my own views in "modern" philosophy of mind. For "modern" the issue essentially is. This is exactly my point here—the very *language* of this dispute traps us with issues that have become fundamental since Kant but that I do not see at all as live when we consider a variety of thinkers from Aristotle to Descartes (and all the way to Hume). I would like to avoid the faux pas I see a lot of us moderns fall into in reading Descartes with a Kantian philosophical grammar.

Where Does Representationalism Come From?

Where is the representationalism I am focused on coming from? In my view, we are led to the form of representationalism by approaching the *informational channel* from sun to mind in the following way. We *carve out* the one last segment in the long efficient causal process—the *internal representation*—to enable us to make it the *bearer of content*, the descendant of the ancient key-to-cognition idea of *form*—that *in virtue* of which we are to avoid being cognitively blinded. And so, the representational content becomes the (latent) separatist dualist's way of discerning us humans from all other sun-processors. We do not merely *exchange* photons with the sun—as rocks and flowers and cats and brutes do—we are the only *thinkers* of the sun.

We can say on behalf of the representational content theory that the long chain from the sun to my brain is external and is merely the *means*. The predicative content-bearing idea or sense or concept of the sun the chain induces is internal (even if, as in modern works prompted by Tyler Burge, individuated by "external indices"). The representation is this internal item that is the very object—what may well be called the *cognitive elixir*—without which there'd be no cognition. "There'd be no" is not meant here merely in the "weak" sense of "causally required background conditions." It is meant in the *logically* constitutive sense: the quantification over this new object—the representation—is part of the very *analysis* of the thinking bond. The representation is not merely the enabler—as it were, the activating enzyme—of the two-place (the sun and me) thinking relation; it is logically *part* of what must be by its very *category*—a *cognitive* relation—a three place relation. Thinking and kicking are logically segregable into different categories.

As I said earlier, Descartes had no place for an internal/external distinction, with the efficient causal chain carved as "external" and the critical segment infused with predicative content as "internal." On my reading of Descartes, there is no external/internal segregation and, in turn, no logical segregation of thinking away from kicking. Just as the kicking of the soccer ball is wholly in nature, the information channel between the sun and mind is *wholly* in nature, with both ends, the sun and me (my mind included), wholly in nature. The thinker, the object thought of, and the thinking-field in between them, the channel, are *all* nature-made.

Fair enough; Descartes does not presuppose an internal/external distinction and, in tow, an internal representing-idea vs. the external-represented sun. But we might wonder—what drives the many representationalists to their classification of the content-bearer (some say "vehicle") *in contrast* to items of the external world, like the sun?

Fourth Principle: Thinking-about Precedes Knowing-which

There is a long tradition in the philosophy of mind that views our knowing which thing x is as a precondition of our being in a position to think about x. Perhaps its most famous recent formulation is by Bertrand Russell (who saw himself often as a "Cartesian" and is described by many as bringing Cartesian themes to the modern arena). Russell says:[5]

> (RP) We cannot be thinking about x unless we know which thing x is.

It has been tempting for many to read Descartes in this fashion—we can think of the sun only because we know which thing it is. When shown that Descartes is quite adamantly arguing to the contrary in the case of our thinking of mundane objects like the sun—as we will see in a moment in his fifth principle—the principle is still attractive to many. They restrict it to (Descartes' account) of our thinking of less mundane objects: God, the self, triangles. It is only because we *know which* thing each of these objects is, that we can *think* about it.

Nothing could be farther from Descartes' view (and the case of God will drive this home). The two kinds of *predicative profiles* Descartes mentions us as having vis-à-vis the sun are both *false* of it: the phenomenal profile "large orange ball in the morning sky" misdescribes that star; and the theoretical profile—giving us its mechanical-gravitational features (according to Descartes' celestial mechanics)—is also *false* of it. These are the profiles we have "inside" our heads; this is what we'd say (in 1641) if asked "So, what is the sun?" We do not *know* which thing the sun is, unless we start calling *false* predicative beliefs, *knowledge*. And yet, false beliefs and all, we—seventeenth century and modern day observers alike—successfully think of the sun (and, of course, Descartes did, too).

Thinking-about versus Knowing-which II: God versus Man (as Thinkers)

It is common in contemporary philosophy of mind to say that whereas God can think of objects "neat" or "directly," I can only think of them as thus and such, in a certain *way*, represented *as* an *F* or a *G*. . . . And so we are back here with predicative representationalism. For man (and other such finite beings) representationalism is inescapable. In contrast, God thinks of things directly.[6]

I would like it noted that the thesis we confront here is not the following "inevitable" thesis we encountered above: whenever I think, I think in a certain way (just as when I touch, I touch in some way or other). The inevitable thesis is really two theses in one. First, the *general necessity* thesis: it must be the case that when I think of the sun, I think in a certain way (or other), though no *particular* way is forced on my thinking. Which brings us to the second, stronger, thesis of *specific necessity*: there is a *specific* way which I am forced to employ if I am to think of the sun. We may hear the two readings by displacing the site in the sentence where the adverbial modifier "necessarily" applies: (i) Necessarily, if I think of the sun, I think in a certain way (general necessity); vs. (ii) A certain way is such that it is necessarily employed in my thinking of the sun (specific necessity). Either way, these necessities are *not* those the contemporary philosopher of mind is focused on. For the necessities I just mentioned apply to God as they apply to us—an activity, involving essentially a relation the sun, has its necessary preconditions. The necessities mentioned so far do not tell us apart from God because they do not arise from the nature of the *thinker(s)*; they rather arise from the nature of the *activity*, whoever (whatever) the nature of the agent is—for anyone to think (see, touch . . .) such and so must happen. . . .

The theses about *ways of thinking* (but not the ways of touching) that are of interest to the modern philosopher of mind do draw invidious distinctions between God and man because they arise from the peculiar nature of the *thinker*. So, now we are not bringing out what the world must be like for *some thinking* to occur; we are bringing out what it is for a *human agent* to be thinking (as opposed to an angel or God or dogs, if only Descartes accorded the latter the capacity).

God's thinking runs quite differently from ours. Of course, he too, and of necessity, in the innocent sense mentioned earlier, does think (and touch) in some way or other. But, unlike me, his way of thinking of the sun does not require subordination to a *way of being given* the sun and with it the application of predicative content to the sun. He does not have to think of the sun *as* an *F* and a *G*... He can just have the brute sun in His mind. For me there is no—and can be no—thinking-of-things without predicative contents applications.

Of course, it is hard to say what God does or can do and it is hard to know how philosophers know His ways so well. So instead of speculative talk about how God does this or that, let me say what I think the key issue here is—those who speak of God's thinking-fashion as opposed to ours propose in effect what I will call the *neat-thinker if and only if omniscient-thinker* bi-conditional:

(O) If one is omniscient vis-à-vis object *x*, one can think directly ("neatly") of object *x*. If one is not omniscient vis-à-vis a certain object *x*, one cannot think of *x* neatly.

(O) is the proposal I would like to focus on because I understand it, unlike other speculations about God's ways. Yet again, Russell may be thought of as an earlier promulgator of this idea, which made him restrict the scope of *our* neat-thinking (we, the non omniscient) to those few items vis-à-vis which we are Godlike, where we know it all. He was assuming that such is our knowledge of our own "sense data" and other totally *transparent* internal phenomena (e.g., famously, Saul Kripke on my own pain).

In contrast, Descartes did not think we are omniscient vis-à-vis our sensations. In spite of a strong press to the contrary, Descartes is no friend of complete-and-perfect knowledge of any subject matter—not about the self, not in mathematics, not about God. We may have a complete *idea of a thing*, a hold in thought of *what* that subject is, but it is not omniscience vis-à-vis all the *truths* about this subject.[7]

Descartes invariantly resists for us humans promises of perfect knowledge of any object x, be x as mundane as the sun or as intangible as the self, a triangle or God. But now, if we hold on to the bi-conditional (O), is not Descartes committed to saying that we, unlike God, cannot neatly think about objects?

Descartes believes (O) is false at the seams. Descartes' contention is that *knowledge*—for that matter, *omniscient or partial*—of the target object is not a prior condition for *thinking* about it (having it in mind). To use "idea" in the technical Cartesian sense, to have an idea of the sun does not require that I have an idea of it in the common parlance sense viz. that first I get some sun-related predicative profile and apply it in thought ("The sun is the object which is F and G and ..."). So thinking about the sun, as neatly and directly as God, does not require from me even mere predicative *beliefs* about x. How can it require true predicative ... *knowledge*, or higher yet, *perfect* knowledge?

Only when the object is *in* our mind, may we predicate *it* in our thinking. This much is true of God just as it is of us—if He does not have some thing in mind, he cannot predicate it in His thinking. Of course, he may have *more* things in mind than I do, being better connected to his creations. So be it. But in Him, as in me, the thinking-about-the-thing comes first. Once He and I have the thing in our respective minds, He can see through it, whereas all I may laboriously gain is incomplete knowledge.

In sum, the idea that something is possible, actual, and indeed essential here for God as a *thinker* (as opposed to *knower*) but is essentially barred for us, is denied by Descartes. There are many matters on which Descartes will be the first to accord God powers and mechanisms of action we cannot aspire to. Thinking-about is not one of them.[8]

Fifth Principle: Each Thinking Is What It Was
Made to Be (By Its Efficient Cause)

Descartes' fifth principle addresses the role of the generative efficient process from sun-to-mind in determining *which* specific thinking act the given thinking act is. This broaches a question technical philosophy characterizes as an *individuation* question—how to count the number of thinking acts; what makes for *distinct* thinking acts.

We might suppose, especially if we are steeped in descriptions of cognition evoking the language of "internal" vs. "external" worlds, that what determines which thinking I am engaged in is what *content* I apprehend.

Where does the search for "individuation criteria" for thinking acts come from in the first place? No discussion in this vein occurs in Descartes, and so one wonders: what forces us to worry about segregating *this kind* of thing, thinkings (that are allegedly otherwise indiscernible)? It seems to me the threat is a by-product of the classical meditative content flow diagram we have already attended to—from mind-by-content to the external world. This diagram explains thinking by starting from the "internal world" and its contents and leaping to the "external world" and its vast plurality of distinct objects. If we reread the sentence I just wrote, we can feel it hides a "ticking bomb": the "external" world already has, quite separately from our thinking, a given large plurality of objects, numerically distinct any two of them. Unless the plurality is of a very *manageable* size (a "microcosm"), how can we expect our minds to be so lucky as to come with equally discerning *contents* that will, as luck would have it, segregate for us one-by-one the already distinct external objects? The internal means—the telescoped contents—start at a disadvantage vis-à-vis the uncontrolled plurality of target external objects.

The sense that we are courting trouble here was aggravated for Descartes, who thought of such "contents" rather concretely. For Descartes modeled them (at least initially in meditation I) after *perceptual images*. It occurred to him immediately that it is very likely that two (indeed, many) worldly objects could be equal candidates for matching, by "resemblance," the content of a given picture-image. At least at first blush, our (imagistic) contents seem ill suited to be individuative, segregative enough, of worldly objects.[9]

Content theory may—and in modern times did—try to catch up with the variety of objects by indexing the contents by "external" information: we build into the content a parameter, enough to segregate among look-similar satisfiers of the internal given content. We must take notice here of a basic point: even if indexed content theory counts target contents more finely, it preserves the very *mechanism* of thinking of its classical non indexed ancestor. With both, we start from inside the mind and content apprehension; we then test for resemblance ("matching") between the contents and worldly objects (the satisfying "denotations"). In indexed-content theories, we amend the mechanism by injecting into the insegregative contents discerning parameters. We serve ourselves de facto to what is de jure taboo information on the classical view, namely the causal process by which the content arose historically in my mind. This is a fact that, speaking de jure, is merely *accidental* on the classical view.

So much for content theories, early and late. Unlike Frege and modern content of thought theorists, Descartes did not have an individuation problem with "from the inside" insegregable thinking acts. Descartes had no such puzzle waiting in the wings. The mechanism that made the sun be in my mind (made me have it in mind) is the one explaining *which* having in mind it is: the one in which the sun came to be in my mind by this intracosmic process. The process that brought the thinking-state into *existence* determines inter alia its distinct *identity* (and thus, individuation).

Descartes' Two Fundamental Corollaries: Existential and Predicative High Risks

Two general and, at that, fundamental, results are pointed out by Descartes in his discussion of the sun. They are claims he had been working on already in Meditation I, and both will turn out to be key pieces of his refutation of skepticism (we will get to this later, in chapter 6). Both are *impossibility* results regarding the mechanism of thinking of objects, the workings of the *cognitive bond*. The first result is this—the mechanism of thinking of objects cannot work by (satisfaction of, resemblance to) predicative contents. I often think of a given target object *x*, be it the sun or myself or, as I will discuss in a moment, God, even though the predicates I ascribed those targets in the head are all wrong. Let us call this the *predicative high risks of thinking*. The second result concerns the *existence* of the target item and its effect on our thinking. If I do successfully think of some object *x*, for example the sun, then the sun exists. Contrapositively put, if the sun hadn't existed, I wouldn't be in a position to think of it. Thus, there is no having in mind of what does not exist. Let us call this *the existential high risks of thinking*.

For Descartes, thinking is always taking high risks. But there are also high gains. The high gains show in Descartes' focus in meditations II, III and VI on what I shall call *reflection conditionals*:

(R) If I think of the sun (God, myself, etc.) then the sun (God, myself, etc.) exists.

Read contrapositively, the conditional asserts: if the sun (God, etc.) does not exist, I am not (and *can* not be) thinking of it. I call the conditionals *reflective* because they bring out how *thinking*-facts reflect the structure of the cosmos proper, that is, existential thinking-*free* facts: my thinking of *x* is only possible because *x* is there. There where? There, first and foremost, in the cosmos and only, in turn, there, in my mind.

The reflection conditional just stated could, of course, be read disjunctively in the form of the high risks dilemmas: either we are not thinking successfully at all of some target object *x* or else we do, and then it follows, from our sheer successful thinking, that *x* exists. If we substitute God for *x*, we are told (i) either that, in spite of our intellectual and psychological involvement for millennia "in this matter," we do not succeed in thinking about God at all, (ii) or else we do and He exists. To which claim I now turn.

FOUR

Thinking about God (and Nature-as-a-Whole)

In this chapter, I would like to understand Descartes' view of another single thinking fact, *my thinking of God*.[1] Essential to such an understanding is Descartes' use of the *reflection conditionals* mentioned in the previous chapter, claims of the form *If I think of God, then God exists,* which we should read contrapositively to feel the bite: *If God doesn't exist, I am not thinking of Him.*

Central to Descartes' account in Meditation III of my think-ing of God is an attempt to *prove* from (i) this thinking fact (ii) a thought-*free* fact about the cosmos, God's existence, or in the more telling gerund form, the fact of *God's existing.* In the *Meditations* there are at least three separate proofs of this (purported) basic fact. In Meditation V, there is an attempted proof of *God's exist-ing* from God's essence (from his true and immutable "nature"). I will call it the *from His essence* proof. In Meditation III, there are (at least) two other proofs. There is a proof of the claim of *God's existing* from *my (JA's) existing.* I will call it the *from my exist-ence* proof. Finally, there is an attempted proof of *God's existing* from this thinking-fact, *I think about God. I* will call it the *from my thinking* proof.

All three proofs are, in my view, extremely interesting in different ways. There are different manners of classifying the three proofs. We may—unifying Meditation V and III—classify together as *thought (cognition)-free* proofs, the from His essence and from my existence proofs. On the other hand, we may classify together as a proof from one *existence to another,* and indeed both appear together in III, the from my existence proof and the from my thinking proof. These two proofs are from one *existence* fact (the existence of myself or of a specific thinking act of mine) to another *existence* fact (the fact of God's existing). Classified this way, the two proofs contrast with the famous ("ontological") proof of Meditation V. The proof in V is not one from existence-to-existence (relating *distinct* real cosmic existences) but a proof from the *essence* (*nature*) of one fixed entity to *its* existence.[3]

Our focus in the present chapter is one proof only: from my thinking of Him to His existence. This will involve for us three facts. First, the reflection conditional—*If I think of Him, He is.* As mentioned late in chapter 3, I call such conditionals *reflection conditionals* because they submit that His existence is *reflected* in my mind's thinking. We can think of my mind as a footprint-filled garden where nature's objects have left their traces.

The second relevant fact is the antecedent of the reflection conditional, the fact that *I think of God*. I will call it the *thinking premise*, an alleged datum regarding what we are thinking—what we have in mind. Finally, there is the consequent of the conditional, *God's existing*, which I will call the *cosmic consequent*, because it is a thought-*free* fact about what there is in the cosmos.

In all, we are interested below in the just-mentioned *reflection arguments* displaying the following *modus ponens* structure:

[R] I think of God (the sun, etc); if I think of God (the sun, etc.), then God (the sun, etc.) exists; therefore, God (the sun, etc.) exists.

We should recall that our main concern in this book is not to prove that He (or the sun or myself, etc.) exists, so much as to understand what is (the nature of) thinking. It is my sense that Descartes' discussion of the thinking premise *I think of God* is deeply revelatory of various themes in his theory of thinking. So our prime interest here is thinking-bound—what kind of fact our premise fact *I think of God* is and what it reveals about thinking. But I will not resist commenting on the conclusion he draws from this fact, the cosmic consequent-fact of *God's existing*.

Let us suppose, for a moment, that Descartes' *modus ponens* arguments did work and their consequents were actually true. After all, there are other arguments of this type of structure that do preserve truth; for example, *I think of the sun* (true); *If I think of the sun, then the sun exists* (true-by-Descartes'-lights); therefore, *the sun exists*. What do we learn here? That a certain *object*, the sun, exists. However, as we saw in the previous chapter, it may turn out that we are seriously *predicatively* wrong about the very *object* about whose existence we just learned. Could this situation come up in the case of God? We'd then have at hand the result—this *object*, God, exists all right—but we'd be substantially predicatively wrong about it, wrong about *how* it was—its modes. Worse, we'd be wrong about *what* it was, its nature.

To repeat, a key question arises at this juncture: assuming we'd prove Descartes' consequent—*God exists*—what exactly would we learn from it?

Much depends on our *understanding* of this consequent. Speaking for myself (rather than Descartes) for a moment, I believe that a proper understanding of what Descartes is after with this consequent-fact provides us, at the same time, with:

(i) something that is *fundamentally true* about the structure of nature (by "fundamentally true," I mean both true and fundamental)

and yet,

(ii) Descartes cannot quite get everything he *wanted* from this true-consequent fact

The clash between (i) and (ii) leads Descartes to recognize what I formulate as a dilemma, a *limitative result*, that reflects something more general about thinking of *things*, not just of God. The limitative result questions whether we can, in one fell swoop, (a) guarantee that we think of a real *thing* (a real *being*), as opposed to thinking merely of a structural *predicate* (a definitive essence-nature) and, at the same time, (b) guarantee that the real thing thought-of satisfies some *definitive predicates* (has a certain *prescribed* predicative essence). It is conjectured below that we must face a hard choice, a kind of Sophie's choice for the believer. I will indeed call the dilemma *the believer's choice*:

> [BC] We are forced to make a choice between (i) thinking of a real being-but-with-no-self-evident (technically: a priori guaranteed) predicative-essence and (ii) thinking of a self-evident (a priori guaranteed) predicative-essence but no guaranteed real thing *whose* essence it is.

The either/or just stated about thinking-of-God amplifies our earlier conclusion, at the end of chapter 3, where we witnessed, with Descartes' high-risks, high-gains dilemma, the clash between real cognitive contact and predicative control. Put in these terms, Descartes' limitative result is that if we seek cognitive contact with the real being God, we cannot guarantee predicative control over His attributes. If we would rather have a "by definition" predicative control, we jeopardize our real cognitive contact with that very being Himself.[4]

To summarize: perhaps Descartes cannot quite secure everything he would have liked to secure from the conclusion *God exists*; perhaps the God that will be shown to exist is not one's desired object of worship, in the sense of (read now in one deep breath) an object-guaranteed-to-have-all-the-attributes-that-made-me-seek-it. These limitations may seem disappointing to the believer, though one's love for far more local (and "controllable") items—one's kids, one's lovers, and so forth—should have already taught one that if it is *real-love* (love of a specific real thing), it cannot be love of a guaranteed cluster of qualities and if one primes the latter kind of love, one may well not (ever!) love a real specific thing.

Be all that as it may, let me say here outright, in view of many derisive modern comments on his proof, that Descartes' launches here a real proof, as good a proof as any ("mathematical") proof

I know, and one revelatory of the most fundamental features of both (i) nature's nature and (ii) our mind's nature.[5]

Intermezzo: The Cognitive Facts versus Our Linguistic Reports

Our focus is this one fact, *I am thinking of God*. This subject-verb-object formulation calls for one final preamble. My concern will be with the worldly fact (if such there be) that I, JA, think of Him, God. Since we are a bit in the dark about whether there is such a fact, such an *actual* relation, let us take a case where we are not in the dark—my thinking of the sun. My point is that I am interested in the cosmic nexus *me-thinking-the-sun*, not the linguistic subject-verb-object *report* sentence "I (JA) think(s) of the sun."

Our concern is the fact that I think of the sun, not what makes the report sentence "I think of the sun" true. In the same vein, my concern here is to understand Descartes on the alleged fact that I am thinking of Him, God; I am not here bent on vindicating the truth of reports like "I think of God" and "The Greeks worshipped Zeus and the Romans worshipped him too." This last report sentence is definitely true not because Zeus/Jupiter *exists(-ed)*. So here we have a true report and even a phenomenon of cofocus (of the Greeks and the Romans) but there is no *object* thought of, and thus no relational fact Greeks-Worship-Object (Zeus).[6]

Descartes' Account of *I think of God*

Descartes' account of this fact—my thinking of Him—is as simple as it is startling. First, for Descartes, this is a given fact of nature we start from, just as, in the previous chapter, we started with my thinking of the sun. It is important to keep in mind that Descartes does not think there is such a fact simply because I assert "I think of God." As he points out, many false-gods-worshippers and other idol-followers make this assertion; their assertion is no evidence that they enter the thinking relation with the one and only true God.

Second, the objectual structure of the fact involves nothing but me and Him. It consists of God's having a secondary mode of being, being in my mind. He always had the first—being in the world. Now that I think of him, have him in my mind, he comes to have the second kind of mode of being. This is well reflected in what I called in chapter 2 the passive form *God is thought of by me* or, in my explicit notation for the fact's structure, *God/thinking$_{JA}$*.

Third, as a consequence of this analysis, it follows that God himself *is*: if He is in my mind, has the secondary mode of being, He is *tout court*, has the primary mode of being. In my view, this is the full Cartesian argument. By this I do not mean to depreciate Descartes' point. To the contrary—its simplicity makes it all the more remarkable.[7]

Here is Descartes' summary:[8]

> The whole force of the argument lies in this: I recognize that it would be impossible for me to exist with the kind of nature I have—that is, having within me the idea of God—were it not the case that God really existed.

On which he amplifies in the second replies to Mersenne:

> I concede also that "we could form this idea even suppos- ing we did not know that the supreme being exists"; but I do not agree that we could form the idea "even supposing that the supreme being did not exist."

Let me say this again (so that perhaps we slowly come to see just how remarkable Descartes' point is). We must remind our- selves that we are focused here on a particular case, God, that makes most of us scientific moderns squirm in our seats (though Descartes, who was as scientific as one could be, did not squirm, and I hope that by the end of this chapter we'll squirm less). We can summarize Descartes' remarkable conjecture by putting it in a disjunctive form: either we are thinking and then thinking of *these* real things (God, the sun, etc.) or else (in these episodes) we are not thinking at all.

Thinking of Unicorns

I spoke of a remarkable conjecture on the part of Descartes. Let us use a modern standard to gauge what is proposed here. Descartes' proposal anticipates (and in my view exceeds in strength in a logical sense to be made clear in a moment) a famous assertion of Kripke's about unicorns.[9] Kripke himself describes this remark as "very surprising" and one that nobody ever believes. Kripke's direct remark is about whether it is *possible* that there would have been unicorns or possible that the planet Vulcan should have existed. Kripke's answer is a sharp *no*, it is not possible. Worse yet, it is not merely impossible, in the sense that the existence of a round square or a reptilian rhinoceros is. In the cases of the unicorns and the planet Vulcan, we don't even have the means (the objects!) to say what the purported state of affairs—state of... *things*, way (mode)... *things* might have been, and so forth—would be. This makes the situation *substantially* (and read the adverb literally) different from the one regarding the merely modal impossibility of satisfying the predicate "is a reptilian rhino." In the latter case, we have the complex property "is a reptilian rhino"; of *it*, we can say that it is not possibly instantiated. The trouble with the unicorns is that we do not have an analogous property "is a unicorn." It is no help to say that the alleged possibility is one in which there are animals looking like horses with one horn in their forehead. This is indeed a possibility but it is not that of *unicorns*, those *specific* animals, existing.

For consider, says Kripke, the existence of these other specific real animals, *the tigers*. They are (i) specific and (ii) real animals. Their existence is not the mere existence of large striped four-legged predators. In the same vein, the existence of *unicorns* is not the mere existence of unicorn look-alikes.

Very well then, we must come with a *structural* enough predicative content, one that runs "deep" and *defines* the unicorns (in the sense of offering modally correct necessary and *sufficient* conditions, adequate for any *possible* situation). Of course, in the case of unicorns such structural-genetic information ("species with DNA *D*") is too late to formulate now. But what about the periodic table's transuranium elements, such as roentgenium, whose structural description (atomic number 111) in the periodic table is indeed modally sufficient?[10]

The Predicative Definitionalist versus the Real
Being and Nothing But

Many read Kripke as saying that if we had such a structural defining predicative content, we'd have *that* missing item (species, atomic element, planet, etc.). I never read Kripke this way because I did not read him as a *predicative definitionalist* on the standard case of the tigers. I read Kripke as telling us that the tigers are *real* and specific, indeed, specific *because* they are real. There is a real species of tigers, generated by the existence of these interbreeding animals and it is *its* reality that guarantees its distinct identity ("specificity").

What is missing in the unicorns case is that *real* species. Predicative content, superficial or structural, cannot masquerade as a real-being of nature—if one had not *come into* nature by one of its natural efficient processes, one cannot *subsequently* exist *in* nature. Whether nature or God are one (on which more below), Descartes emphasizes in both Meditation III and in his reply to Burman that whatever has being has been (i) *getting* that being from nature/God, (ii) by a *process* of cosmic nature that results in (iii) the being's be-ing in the image of God (nature), a microcosm as it were[11]:

OBJECTION. Could God not have created you and yet not have created you in His image?

REPLY. No. For it is an axiom, accepted and true, that "the effect is similar to the cause." God is the cause of my being; I am His effect, therefore I resemble Him.

Objection. But a builder is the cause of a house and yet it does not resemble him.

REPLY. He is not the cause in the sense we are here giving to it. He does no more than apply active things to things that are passive; and his work therefore need not resemble him. The cause of which we are speaking is the *causa totalis*, the cause to which the very existence of things is due. Now a cause of this kind cannot produce anything not similar to itself. For since it is itself an existent and a substance and in producing something is calling this something into existence, that is to say is creating something where before there was nothing whatsoever (a mode of production proper only to God), this something must at least be an existent and a substance, and so thus at least be in the similitude and image of God.

OBJECTION. But if so a stone and all other things will be in the image of God.

REPLY. They too will have His image and similitude but very remote, exiguous and confused; whereas I, to whom God in creating me has given me more than to other things, am thereby the more in his image.

For Descartes, beings—stones, houses, men—are *brought about* by such (total) causes. Defining predicates, structural as they might be, are not be-ings and not inserted into history by causal-generative processes.

The talk of "defining" beings is misleading if by *definition* we mean something that *brings* an entity into existence. No definition has that power. Of course, if by definition we mean rather what perhaps Aristotle meant (subsequent *description* of the fundamental features of an antecedently existing phenomenon), I would have no qualms with "animals of DNA T" read as a definition (that is, a fundamental description) of the species of tigers. But it is a definition not because it brought the species into the world; it is rather the other way round: the species, by existing and having some fundamental features, engendered *its* real definition, understood now as—its deep *description*.

The real definition of being *B* is now read as photograph of *B*, except that unlike an ordinary photograph of *B*, it "X-rays" *B*'s *structure* rather than representing *B*'s phenomenal look. And we all know the facts of photographing—it is not the X-ray photograph that gave rise to the patient (e.g., the tigers); it is the patient that gave rise to the—*its own*—X-ray photograph.

Essence (Nature) of . . .

Armed with these distinctions, we may revert to the classical essence/existence terminology. We need to separate two—the *prefabricated* and the *generated*—readings of the phrase "essence of tigers" (and, in time, "essence of God"). On the one reading, the essence is a structural predicative content and it exists prior to and independent of the goings on in the forests of the world; the real tigers are then *of* the essence, are *instantiations* of the antecedently given predicate. This order fits what I called an argument *from essence* (given antecedently) *to existence*, as the argument in Meditation V seems to read.

The orthogonal understanding of "essence of . . ." reads *essence of* on the model of an X-ray photograph of a being *B*. The existence of *B* is prior, and *B*'s coming into being engenders its essence (there is no *B* without *B*'s essence but also vice versa—no *B*'s essence without *B*). It is this last reading I used to give to Kripke on tigers: they—the species they make—*engender* the essence of the species. Since there are no unicorn-animals and thus no living species of unicorns, there is no essence there-*of*.

On the generative reading of Kripke, it is not simply that there is no unicorn-*possibility*. Nothing I *conceive* (imagine, think of) is described correctly as my having conceived-of-(etc.)-unicorns. We are thus trapped by Descartes' stark disjunction: either we think of *it* (*them*) or we do not, in this case, successfully think at all.[12]

It is possible to read Descartes as a predicative definitionalist and one priming prefabricated essences. On this analysis, the fact Descartes is so keen on—my thinking of God—is not in the end a structure-mate of this other fact, my thinking of the sun. In the latter, it is the real sun (and nothing but it) that enters my mind, it is only *its* secondary mode of being that makes the fact obtain. Not so in the case of God. What I am related to is a complex predicate, if you will, a prefabricated predicative "true and immutable nature." When I think of God, I think of—any old thing *as long as it satisfies the defining predicate.*

And so, there is no way for someone (not even...God!) to come up to me and say: you are indeed thinking of the satisfier of this defining predicate but you are not thinking of the real entity, you are not thinking of *me,* simply because it turns out that that real entity—me, says God—does not satisfy the predicate. This "turn out false" scenario, which we examined late in chapter 3, is precisely what could and *did* happen with the sun. The sun simply showed up and said: you have been thinking of me, René Descartes, but actually I, the sun, do not satisfy the structural physical predicate of your gravitation theory, Descartes (or for that matter, the theories of Newton or Einstein either).

This possibility of the real entity turning out to escape its alleged definition simply cannot arise on the predicative definitionalist reading—to be God is simply to be whatever satisfies the predicative definition.

The *Real Being and Nothing But* Reading of Descartes

On this second reading, Descartes treats *I think of God* just as he treats *I think of the sun.* Indeed, why else would he have launched into a long discussion of thinking of the sun and of the phenomenon of coldness, if when we move to the case of God, our thinking is suddenly not real-phenomenon-bound but is rather after surrogate predicative contents? For Descartes, God (and if not by this name than by any other we may stipulate) is first and foremost a *real being*. For Descartes, He is more real than any other real being—it is He in virtue of whom all the rest of us beings get their respective degree of being (reality). I do not want to belabor the point of what Descartes was "really after," but this one—in thinking of God, it is of a *real being* that I think—is very obvious in his writings.

Should we say then that hand in hand with this objectual reading of *I think of God* comes—as in thinking of the objectual sun— the threat of a *predicative confusion*: I am thinking of the being God all right, but I may well turn out (am bound to be) confused about its features?[13]

Thinking of Nature-as-a-Whole versus Thinking of God

Recall now Descartes' claim about God and nature in Meditation VI (CSM II, 54):

> Nature considered in its most general aspect...I understand by the term nothing other than God himself or the ordered system of created things established by God.

There are two interesting possibilities of interpretation of the relationship between God and nature, as described here. The one is *identity theory*—nature-as-a-whole (the ordered system...) is one and the same as God. Call this the *identity theory*. The second reading is the *creator theory*: nature-as-a-whole is established/created by God.

Now, nature-as-a-whole exists. Suppose, with the identity theory, that, our awareness notwithstanding, in thinking of nature as a whole, we think of God. Then, in turn, in thinking of God, and again our awareness aside, we do indeed think of God. Let this for a moment be stipulated as the true metaphysical state of things (this is how *things* are, in particular *these* things). I would like us to see now how—in this kind of setup—we could be thinking of God but be radically wrong about Its (= His) predicative features.

Of course, Descartes may not adhere to the identity theory of God I just stipulated. Descartes does seem rather an adherent of the creator theory. But recall also that Descartes is bound by the following desiderata: (i) he would like to preserve the mundane fact that I think of—have in mind—God; (ii) he would like this to be explained uniformly by his overall account of thinking, his overall intracosmic efficient causation principle of transmission from the object thought of to me. Can he satisfy these desiderata?

Descartes' situation reminds one of an analogous setup (of course on a more local scale) regarding our thinking of—persons.[14] One metaphysical theory is that a given person, JA, is identical with its human body, which by Descartes' own light, is not just this or that pile of molecules. As argued in *WAI* (following Descartes' 1645 letter to Mesland), the piles change but I have one and only one body throughout my existence. I am essential to it and it is essential to me. So one hypothesis here is that where JA is the person and JB is my body, JA = JB. This is the identity theory (of persons). Of course, some (Descartes included) do not believe the identity theory. Descartes might (and *does*, on my reading of him; see *WAI*) take JA and JB as essentially *connected*, but numerically and categorically distinct (the one is a person, the other the body of a person, etc.). Let this be. We can now consider the question: what is going on when someone thinks of the person JA?

A natural way to proceed for Descartes is to separate in his account two steps. The target is to show that if you think of JA, if you have me-JA in mind, then I-JA exist (I have in addition to the secondary also the primary mode of being).

How would he describe things here?

First, Descartes would isolate the *causal transmission step: If* you successfully think of JA, you must have been thinking of JB, because you must have had JB in your mind—it is energy from JA's body, that is, from JB, that forged a causal process all the way to your brain and, through it, to your mind. Of course, you may have never said "I think now of JB" (you might have even said: I don't give a damn about JB, I think now of JA, for example, as a purely moral agent, etc.). Nonetheless, to think of JA you must have JB in mind, for this is how—and *only* how—information from JA starts its long journey to you.

So, if you think of JA, you think (en route) of JB. This much is the *causal step*. If we believe the identity theory, we are done. Thinking of JB is, inter alia, thinking of JA. But suppose that, like Descartes, we don't believe the identity theory of persons (as I do not). We now need to argue—and this second step I call *the essentialist step*—that JB's very identity, what specific thing it is, is to be the body of JA (this indeed is Descartes' theory in the 1645 letter to Mesland, analyzed in *WAI*). There is no thinking of JB without thinking of JA because to have JB in mind is to have—*the body of JA* in mind. Why? Because *what* JB is, is just that—the body of JA. Once you are having in mind JB, you are having me, the person, in mind—there is no sense of existence and identity for JB without the genitive construction: it is that *person's*, JA's, body.[15]

I suggest that a similar approach may help square Descartes' plurality of desiderata regarding our thinking of God. To remind us: the target is to draw from *I think of God* the conclusion *God exists*. In the first *causal* step, we sort out what it is to have the right cosmic causal process that would put God in my mind; this much must go through the cosmos as a whole, the (at the very least) material manifestation of God. So we cannot be thinking of God unless we think of (have in mind) nature as a whole. If we believe the identity theory, we are done by this stage: Unbeknownst to us, we are thinking of God (and God exists).

But suppose that, like Descartes, we hold on to the creator theory. It is incumbent on Descartes to argue now, in a second step, the *essentialist* step, that the very whatness of the cosmos, that as it were all there is to its being is "the universe created by God." If this much is arguable, Descartes could conclude that thinking of nature as a whole *requires* us, in turn, to think of what it essentially is—the universe created by God. And so, God is in my mind and God exists.

I believe Descartes *must* hold on to the first causal step if he is to offer a uniform theory of having in mind things, by efficient causal processes. And I think he *does* believe in the first step. He surely seems to believe in the second step—the essentialist premise—regarding what the nature of nature-as-a-whole is. Indeed, a stronger claim may be made on behalf of Descartes (recalling here the dialog with Burman about the stone in the image of God, quoted earlier): in every thinking episode of mine, be it about myself, the stone, the sun, and so forth, I think of nature as a whole (for it is in the nature-whatness of each such nature-product to be nature's product). And thus, if Descartes is right about nature's own nature (what it is), in every episode of thinking, I think about God. And so, Descartes could well conclude that not only is God-thinking reflecting God's existence; there is no thinking, of any thing whatsoever, without God-thinking.[16]

FIVE

Descartes' Cosmological Invariants I: Thinking

We have looked at some paradigm cases of Descartes' account of thinking. We are in a position to distill some general *structural* features of Descartes' relation of *thinking about*. Understanding what it takes for us to be thinking (and how we know that we are), leads Descartes, in turn, to an account of the structural features of another fundamental cognitive relation, that of *knowing*. Conventionally, we call the first type of investigation "metaphysics" (of thinking), the second "epistemology."[1]

This dualism of metaphysics and epistemology is not the way Descartes cuts the pie. For him, there is just an investigation of the *nature* of this or that cognitive relation. Following this approach, the present chapter focuses mainly on structural features of thinking-facts, the next one on those of knowing.

Cosmic Invariants of Thinking-about

Following Descartes, we have focused in the previous chapters on direct object-facts of the form:

JA—Thinks of—The Sun

Three constituents are involved in such facts: the agent-thinker, the activity, and the object-of-the activity. This threefold structure suggests that we can distill various kinds of structural features of thinking by analyzing a host of pertinent *invariances*. This we do by altering (permuting) one dimension in the thinking-fact, while keeping the others fixed.

Suppose we removed this particular subject, JA, and focused on the subject-generic:

... —*Thinks of*—*The Sun*

Here we confront marks of *thinking-of-the-sun*, whoever (whatever) is doing the thinking. Let us call such features *subject-invariant*. To give us a feel for such subject-invariants, let us recall that one such invariant we have already encountered in the reflection arguments of chapters 2–4. Let our thinking subject be whoever we'd like him/her to be. Descartes observes now: If he/she is thinking of the sun, the sun exists; or more carefully, at one point in that thinking subject's past, the sun *existed*. Exposing such sun-thinking *subject-invariants* is Descartes' method of unraveling *structural* features of sun-thinking, features that govern *any* subject's sun-thinking.

We could, of course, permute in our original fact the object position item by considering:

JA thinks of—...

We are now focused on the (distinct) marks of JA's thinking episodes, whoever (whatever) is the object thought of by JA. I will call such (thinking-subject-fixed, here JA) marks *object-invariants*. Such invariances turn out to be revelatory of structural features of *this* man's, JA's, thinkings.

Generalizing further, we may simultaneously permute both the object and subject position items and so isolate the invariances of the very activity, the thinking-period, so to speak, whoever the subject and whatever the object. I will call such marks *generic-thinking invariants*. With such invariants we may edge toward the fundamental structural features of the activity itself: thinking, wherever and whenever it takes place.

Finally, we may even consider, as Descartes surely did, an alteration of the so-far fixed *activity*—thinking. We may be interested in isolating the structural features of *cognitive* activities such as thinking, imagining, willing, seeing, knowing, and other such. We may be comparing cognitive activities—any of the foregoing—with noncognitive activities (or goings-on) such as JA's crashing (his spaceship) into the sun or falling into the Amazon River. One such comparison shows up in Descartes' (and Pierre Gassendi's) contrasting of the facts of *my* (JA) *thinking* and *my* (JA) *walking*.

Let us proceed by laying out, in this order, Descartes' approach to the aforementioned types of invariants.

Object, Subject, and Activity Invariants

On the reading we have developed in chapters 2–4, there are ways—general *logical* ways of the thinking relation, *whatever* kind of item we slot in as the object of thinking-relation—in which thinking about the sun, about oneself, about God, and about the plurality of material things are similar: all are (meant to be) thinkings about real natural phenomena. It was thus that we discussed *reflection arguments*, where regardless of what-*x*-is, Descartes said: I think of *x*; if I think of *x*, then *x* exists; therefore *x* exists.

As mentioned throughout chapters 2, 3, and 4, this reflection argument involves hidden dark corners. The *modus ponens* I just recited does seem to work out for my thinking of God or of the sun. But for this to work out at all, Descartes needs to put together more than the *purely logical* features of the thinking relation—*more* than the fact that *x* existed at one point in the past. For Aristotle surely existed in the past, but from my thinking of him now, it should not follow that he exists now.

Enter now, in addition to the general logical features of thinking, specific *essentialist* factors, induced by the specific *nature* or *kind* of phenomenon thought of. Here we expect differences between thinking of the sun, of oneself, of God, and the plurality of material things, if only because these objects simply qua objects (*before* anyone thinks of them) differ in kind. By putting together the logical and the essentialist features, we can formulate Descartes' theory of *thinking-invariants*—those dependency-factors underlying our episodes of thinking.

Let us see how this works out in specific cases.

On the front of purely *logical* invariants, as emphasized, I see Descartes as embracing what was called *reflection arguments*:

[R] I think of the sun (God, etc.); if I think of the sun (God, etc.), then the sun (God, etc.) existed; thus, the sun (God, etc.) existed.

Suppose we grant Descartes his account of what was just called the logical profile of the thinking-relation as embedded in reflective arguments of the [R] type. All we'd get from the truth of a premise of the form *I think of x* is an *efficient-causation* driven invariant:

(EC) x, the object of my current thinking, must have existed, at one point in the past, a point at which an efficient causal path was initiated from x and onto the (my) present thinking episode.

Of course, the target object *x*, for example the sun, does not come cosmos-free. For the sun to have existed, a whole chain of beings beforehand had to-be-in-order. Only with that *genealogical tree* in order, *that* star formation could come about. And so, if I think now of the sun, by (EC), we get not only that (i) the sun existed at one point in cosmic history, but that (ii) there also existed everything that was essential—all that was sine qua non— for the sun's existence. And so if I now think of the sun, it follows, for example, that the Milky Way existed.

Following Descartes' Meditation III, let us assume (EC). A major problem remains: how do we get from the target object *x*'s past existence to *x*'s *present* existence—for example, to the truth of *God exists* and indeed to *the sun exists*, both conclusions that Descartes would like to draw? How do we make sure *not* to get the false conclusion that just because I now think of Aristotle, he now exists? What is more, there may be a star S (let us leave our sun on the back burner for a moment), of which (i) I am thinking right now; and (ii) light from S to earth travels for, say, a year; (iii) I got light from S sometimes in the past, but (iv) by now S does not (present tense) exist.

It seems then that Descartes' arguments about God and the sun must rest on further hidden premises, conditions not available in the case of Aristotle or the star S. Whatever these extra-conditions are, they will take us away from purely universalizable-logical conditions like (EC). We would rely on more restrictive features having to do with the nature of this *specific* object (e.g., the sun) and its relation to my specific nature (e.g., I, a human being, would not exist *now* (and thus would not be thinking *now* without it).

So, how is Descartes to explain these differences among invariants for sun-thinking? We have a truth-preserving inference from my thinking of God now that God exists now, because, assuming that He existed in the past at all—which He would, by the just cited universal condition (EC), He is the kind of being who would always continue to exist. This last step is *essentialist*—specific to the nature of God. The grounding of the truth-preserving inference from my thinking of the sun to the sun's existing now runs differently. For (as just shown in the case of star S), the sun may have existed in the past but still go out of existence later. No doubt, our sun *will* go out of existence sometimes in the future. But as long as I am thinking, in particular sun-thinking, it must be around. For here we call upon *my* essential features—I (and any other human thinker) would not exist now, if the sun had collapsed by now. The same is true for any human thinker in the past, such as Aristotle: if he thought of the sun on a certain Monday of January 330 BC (using our calendar), the sun existed then, on that Monday. If it had not been in existence then, he would not be there (and then) to think of it. This makes the sun required for any *human* thinking (because required for the thinker's existence).

Could this be pushed farther? Could we substitute for the sun in the *object* position some other target object *x* and still be able to substitute in the *subject* position, me (JA), by any other human thinker, such as Princess Elizabeth or Kate Moss, preserving all the while the present-tense existence conclusion that *x exists*? It may well be argued that, say, my thinking of water is such an example; not my thinking of this or that bit of water but of that very kind of liquid. For if any human being thinks at all, for that matter, thinks of water, that very thinking fact would not hold, if the thinker didn't exist; and the human thinker wouldn't exist, unless water existed to make much of that thinking-man. Thus, for us humans, we can say that there is no thinking of water without water's contemporary existence.

It is natural to wonder further in this vein: could some human thinker truly be thinking of planet earth, thus have it made true by (EC) that the earth *existed*, and yet that it'd be false, by the time of the thinking, that the earth *exists*?

This can surely envisaged as true for future human thinkers who will have resettled on the moon or Mars, making sure, for some reason, to bomb out of existence planet Earth. Indeed, it may be argued that our generation of thinkers already reached that point: Neil Armstrong could well have been thinking of planet Earth while making sure to bomb it out of existence beforehand.[2]

And so it goes. We may, as we just did, vary the *object* of the thinking, while fixing the thinker or kind thereof (mankind). But we may contemplate other variations. We may envisage rather different *kinds* of objects—God, oneself, mathematical items. Alternatively, we may consider other kinds of cognizing *subjects* (beyond the human pool): God and angels on the one hand, brutes and dogs on the other. And finally, we may vary the type of activity concerned—thinking of the wax as opposed to seeing it, imagining the triangle (chiliagon) as opposed to understanding it, sensing the pain in the leg as opposed to intellectually apprehending it, and so forth.

Throughout these variations, it has seemed to many readers of Descartes that by altering the fabric of the target object, or the makeup of the thinking subject or the kind of cognitive activity involved, we would get considerable *freedom* to depart from the ground-zero case of this analysis, the paradigm mentioned early in chapter 2—*my thinking of the sun.* It is often suggested that Descartes is a role model for such a methodology of changing the basic model as we move to hard(-er) cases—vary the "parameters" and you vary considerably, for Descartes, the overall account. Did Descartes not think that dogs and brutes don't *think* at all? And what of very young infants?[23] Furthermore, while we humans are shown in Meditation VI to depend so critically on our senses, do not angels and God display total sense-independence? What is more, does not Descartes submit that while efficient information from the sun is constitutive to my having the sun in mind, no such energy transfer is even *possible* when I think of myself or God or triangles?

Well, yes, variations in the parameters make for a difference. If the target object is immaterial, as, for example the mathematical kind of triangle is, photons (light) wouldn't bounce from its surface (but we must stop and wonder, is the kind *tigers* any less abstract and immaterial? It too does not reflect photons, even if individual tigers do). And yes, Descartes does famously say that (i) dogs don't think at all and (ii) angels apprehend their pain in quite a different way from us, humans, who are made of an *intermingled* mind and body. It might seem that categorical differences arise, once we go beyond the simple model where (i) the object of cognition is the material sun, (ii) the thinking subject is a visually-equipped cognizer, and (iii) the cognitive activity is very strongly founded (or is identical with) visually-seeing the sun. Intangible objects and differently equipped subjects make a marked difference; and different activities (thinking vs. imagining vs. willing vs. sensing) have different ranges as their accessible domains.

To all of this, I would like to say, Yes, some of the differences Descartes marks are shining examples and they raise interesting issues. But even when the differences shine, they are, in my view, outshined by Descartes' insistence to subsume them all under the fundamental and unificatory explanation of cognition. In cognition, we have a phenomenon *of* nature, wherein the objects and facts of nature impinge on one of its own kind of products, *cognitive agents*, by means of nature-bound information-transmission processes.

I believe that many readers of Descartes have been prey here to the kind of fallacy that Descartes himself warns us against in both the fourth replies (CSM II, 160) and the December 1640 letter to Regius (CSM III), in the mind/body case (a fallacy that many indulge in anyway and which I analyze in detail in *WAI*). In his letter to Regius and his remarks in the fourth replies on the arm–body connection, Descartes insists, no doubt about it, on the separation of mind and body. But he *only* does that in order to bring out how much of *one* man the separated two are and *essentially* (*"by nature"*) so. Instead, the analytic reader attends to only the first half of Descartes' film—mind and body have been separated! The reader leaves the cinema before the end and draws dramatic conclusions by overemphasizing what was merely one preparatory step of separation in order to unify better.

One could well say that Descartes lived by the maxim *separer pour mieux unifier* (to be read on the model of *reculer pour mieux sauter*). In contrast, the modern analytic reader often separates for distinction's sake and never comes back for the second half of the film. It is my feeling that a similar fallacy recurs in many readers' overemphasis of Descartes' contrast between imagination and thinking, seeing and understanding, and so forth. We forget what the point of the separation was.

To attend to a few often mentioned examples. Granted, Descartes does think that God, self and mathematical items are all not wholly material. But the common view that he consigns them all to another, dual, platonic realm of independent, and not just *im*-material but *anti*-material, items is quite wrong, and wrong about the items *in se* much *before* any cognition of the items comes up.[4]

It is true, of course, that for Descartes the items are not purely extended. But their existence is essentially tied to nature's existence, as indeed the very *category* of existences (beings) is understood by Descartes—to be is to be in and of nature. Thus, whatever object is now to come up is bound *to* nature—as a creator thereof, as the thinking part of a natural man or as the figure and number of natural extended objects. So even before our cognition is investigated, the items proper—God, self, mathematical kinds of objects—have their existence intermingled with that of nature, indeed their very raison d'être is that they are *essential* constituents of that nature, making it as complex as it is.

This much concerns *what* God, selves, and mathematicals are. When it comes to our cognition of these items, it is Descartes' basic idea (we have seen this much in chapters 2–4) that (i) the *nature* of the cognition-of-*x*, is (ii) to track the *nature* of *x*. For example, if the mathematicals are engendered by the geometric and arithmetic features *of* extended things (or the extended realm as a whole), it is no surprise that we cognize *them*—the mathematicals—by having built into us structural features of the extended spatio-temporal universe. Granted, such ideas do not arise in us in the way the idea of a tiger would (recall that this means "the way we come to have tigers in mind"). Perhaps sensory encounters, *during* one's lifetime, will be called upon for tigers-cognition. In the case of triangles-cognition, we may have in mind the kind independently of any particular lifetime sensory experience. But not independently of (i) our living in nature, our being *its* creatures, and of (ii) its material and spatiotemporal infrastructure being what it is. We are nature's products and organs (to be read on the model of: my arm is my body's product and organ). In thinking, we respond to the niche that made us and sustains us. And, on Descartes' cosmological picture in Meditation VI, it is in this *response*—be the response the *seeing* of colors (CSM II, 55), the visual *imagining* and algebraic *understanding* of mathematical figures (CSM II, 53), the *sensing* pain and thirst (CSM II, 57–58)—that cognition consists.[5]

So, to reiterate, the differences between cognition-types are many. There are object-differences when we vary the fabric (kind) of the target thinking-object, as when we move from Aristotle to the sun and on to the triangles and material objects in general. There are also subject-and-activity differences, as when we vary the kind of the thinking subjects or the kind of cognitive activity they undertake.

The point remains: the having in mind of an object works for us all—nature cognizers—by the same mold—the object, itself nature bound, engenders information that reaches our brains by efficient processes and is subsequently processed by our cognizing units. Our brains may be different—inside a given species and across cognizing species—and so are our subsequent cognitive activities. But the sun is one and the same through and through; the light that travels from it is just that—light; the brains that process it are, within certain obvious differences, made of similar light-receptive materials and equipped with information processing capacities, inducing similar images, words, and so forth, inside our cognizing unit. At no stage—and this is the *key* point—an *out of this world*, *hyper* natural, cognitive processing device ("cognizing unit") is invoked for any of us, cognizers. Nor is any out-of-nature process ever called upon to connect the sun with the cognizers. The differences are there, but they are all variations on a theme, the theme manifested in the ground-zero paradigm, *my thinking of the sun.*[6]

Let me emphasize this point, for it is at the basis of the *integration-without-reduction* theme that I submitted early in chapter 1 as a key to Descartes' project. Reduction is through and through anathema to Descartes: thinking is not (not one and the same as) imagining, which is not visually seeing; thinking of the sun is different from thinking of triangles, which is different from thinking of nature-as-a-whole (or God); and so on—what dogs do when they see the sun and have it cognitively in them is not what we do when we think of the sun and subsequently rub our skin with sun-lotion. No reduction then but all the same integration—across all the different kinds of cognizers, different kinds of activities and different kinds of objects cognized, the basic scheme of sun-thinking by that human, JA, offers us the primary mold of cognition in and of nature.

Let me sum up. We have seen that, for Descartes, various kinds of dependencies rein my thinking (e.g., of the sun)—in all such (my, our) thinkings certain preconditions are required and certain invariants recur. We may well separate the invariant-types we discussed in three categories:

(A) *Object-existence*: conditions required for the object of the activity (e.g., thinking), such as the sun's existence.
(B) *Subject-existence*: conditions required for the thinking-subject, such as JA's existence.
(C) *Activity-occurrence*: given the sun's existence and my present existence, we articulate conditions allowing information-transfer from the sun to me, in a way conducive to my specific kind of cognitive *activity*, such as thinking (remembering, imagining, etc.)

All three invariant-types concern *existence*-conditions: what it takes for the world to have certain target-objects, thinking subjects, and cognitive activities. In this respect, the focus of Descartes' invariant types is orthogonal to the one we encounter in classical analysis of thinking along the RC and MF models. For in the classical theories, we demand very little from the world (if anything) for an act of thinking of mine to be possible (or, actual; there is no substantial difference between the two demands). Indeed, as we saw in chapters 1–4, it is the very point of such theories that whether a thought may be had *must* be prior to and independent of what the world is actually like.

A paradigm of this independence is accomplished by the classical "separatist" Cartesian dualist conception in which the thinking subject is a pure Cartesian mind and its contents of thought are all prefabricated; that is, they would be available no matter which world were the world in which the thinking actually took place. But even when it is agreed that some "external" conditions affect the occurrence of my thinking of the sun (e.g., the full man JA has to exist; the Milky Way galaxy had to exist, etc.), the focus of classical accounts is not existence conditions (for the thinking fact) but rather further *internal* cognitive conditions. The critical question becomes: when I think of the sun or of Aristotle or Kate

Moss, what is it that I must know a priori or simply know or have as further thoughts (beliefs), that could *back up* my thinking of these objects?

The classical thought here—whether by way of a representational content fixing my object of thinking or a *form* allowing my mind to understand it (making it intelligible to my mind)— is to analyze my very thinking of the sun (Aristotle, Kate, etc.) as (i) independent of worldly conditions but as (ii) very much dependent on my having a rich cognitive repertoire of predicative knowledge *in virtue* of which my mind is put in contact with these targets. To recall the basic point in chapters 2 and 3, such predicative information is not a by-product (an after-thought, as it were) of the efficient causal link that put the sun (Aristotle, etc.) in my mind—as it were, upon having the sun in mind, it *turns out* that it came packed with predicates such as "massive heavenly object" or "large orange ball on the horizon," and so forth. On the classical models, it is the other way round—it is my thinking the predicative content that makes me come to think of, in due course, its denotation. Thus, the predicative profile I do have in mind first makes it possible to have, and only in this derivative dependent way, the sun itself as a predicatively enveloped cognized object.

On my reading of Descartes, we find the opposite pattern: (i) very little, if any, internal predicative information, about the sun is required for thinking of it, but (ii) thinking does rest on a host of nature-dependent facts without which I would not be engaged in this activity and at that of this specific object, the sun.

So much regards my *thinking* of the sun, and it seems to make no mention of *knowing* anything, not about the sun or myself or the intervening causal media. For all that was said about when and how I think of the sun, I may not know *anything* of nature. Could this be right (as a reading of Descartes)? May I think so successfully of nature yet know none of it? It is to this question that I now turn.

SIX

Descartes' Cosmological Invariants II: Knowing

Descartes' account of thinking made essential use of reflection arguments. We traced in the previous chapter the cosmological invariants underlying any episode of thinking of (i) some specific item x, and (ii) more generically, of any thinking. We saw that from the fact "I am thinking of x," as well as the generalization "I am thinking," much can be squeezed out about nature, simply because if it weren't for these background nature-facts, the emergent fact "I think of x" (and more generally, "I think") would simply not emerge in nature.

Very well, we might say, but what good does this do for us? Our underlying worry here is this. We admit that in nature, facts of the "I am thinking (of x)" kind—the facts proper, never mind how we know them—reflect much of nature's own structure. But, our discomfort goes on, what good are these thinking-facts *for us*, in particular what good are such reflection arguments if we do not *know* the thinking *premises* of these arguments?[1]

Perhaps I can summarize the answer given in our current chapter by this one thought—far from running into an inevitable clash with sound epistemology, Descartes' metaphysics of thinking provides us with light at the other end of the tunnel—an epistemology that is a by-product of his naturalistic metaphysics of thinking. In a nutshell, for Descartes, there is no other a prioristic discipline of "normative Cartesian epistemology." There is simply, all the way down, a metaphysics of cognitive relations. Some cognitions, provided they are properly generated in nature, are thinkings thereof; some cognitions, provided they are properly generated in nature, are knowings thereof; finally, some cognitions, provided they are not only generated by nature but are made by it *of* our nature, are fundamental-structural kinds of knowings.

This one summary thought—it is metaphysics of cognitive relations all the way down—leads us to a methodological reversal in approaching the murky depths of "epistemology."

In speaking of "epistemology" as many of us pursue it, I allude to the following two-tier methodological thesis in the theory of knowledge:

> (i) *Knowledge Dualism*. The theory of mundane knowledge (e.g., I know that snow is white and I have two hands) and the theory of a priori knowledge (I know that I think and that 2 + 2 = 4) are two separate subjects, and they can be developed independently.
>
> (ii) *Apriority First*. The theory of a priori knowledge—with its paradigms of mathematical and self knowledge—is to be attacked first. We focus here on the truths that can be known from the inside, as it were, before having to confront the vicissitudes of interaction with the external world, the reliability of causal mechanisms, normative standards on perceptual evidence, and so forth.

In my view, and as a consequence of his theory of thinking, Descartes questions our standard two-tier thesis. First, for Descartes, there is only one theory—of knowledge of nature. Second, the "elite cases" of God, self, and mathematics emerge as limit cases of the mundane, just more cases of knowing natural facts, whose place (i) in nature and (ii) in our human-nature, is fundamental.[2]

Descartes on Knowing Nature's Facts

The thesis of Descartes emerges in Meditation VI, the optimistic finale of the *Meditations*: If only we understood our place in nature and how we succeed in thinking of it, we'd realize that we know much about nature. This optimistic-sounding "know much about nature" breaks down for Descartes into what I will call Descartes' epistemic quartet:

(E1)   What we know are facts of cosmic nature.
(E2)   We know for certain many cosmic facts.
(E3)   Some facts we know, we know from our own nature, independently of lifetime sensory experiences.
(E4)   We do not know a priori, in the sense of efficient-contact independence, any facts.

We may appreciate that Descartes' epistemic quartet goes way beyond the first-tier high risks/high gains dilemma—one may embrace the first tier and go on to assert that we do not know for certain any cosmic facts. Such a philosopher would have us thinking of real objects but as a result would view us as knowing no cosmic facts for certain.[3]

This pessimism about certain knowledge is far from being Descartes' diagnosis. Indeed, he completes Meditation VI with a revelatory claim in the last paragraph that the dreaming story was hyperbolic—we all know for certain we are awake, when we are. Descartes might seem—and has become to many the paradigm of—a certainty-pessimist, if we confuse two epistemic notions, certainty and apriority. For it is indeed Descartes' claim—see (E4)—that we do not, and cannot, know in a contact-free way any real nature fact. But he does not conclude that we do not know anything for certain. Quite the contrary—many of the cosmic facts we know, we know for certain. And some we know by and from our own nature.

Knowing as Successful Thinking

How are we to understand the basis of Descartes' epistemic quartet? The key lies in (E1). The reasons for (E1) go back to Descartes' theory of thinking, laid out in chapters 2–5. This calls for some explanation.

What does (E1) say? It makes my knowings of, for example, the sun's being large, God's being good, myself walking (thinking), and so forth, a relation between me and a fact. Now, in contemporary "analytic" philosophy, we are prone to discussions between ontology designers ("What do you admit in your ontology?" we say, sounding as if we are asking, "Who did you invite to your party?"). And so, as we invoke a seemingly new category of "things"—facts—some philosophers will fuss about what exactly is the identity of a "fact" and whether we have individuation-criteria for the category; in a nutshell, what is it to have an "ontology of facts."

Descartes does not fuss over this, and following him I will not. We do not need to reify "facts" as some sort mysterious entities (in the vein of "propositions," "thoughts," "contents," etc.). All we need here is Descartes' vernacular-based discussions in the *Meditations*, through which we have gone, emphasizing that it is nature's objects (and, speaking in the gerund form, their being this or that way) that we are thinking of. I think of the sun and, in thinking of it, I sometimes think of its being large. Our practice above, applied to my thinking of the sun, was to bring out the structure of that thinking fact by the notation $Sun/Thinking_{JA}$. By parity of form, I indicate the fact of my knowing the sun's being large by: $Sun's\text{-}being\text{-}large/Knowing_{JA}$. We could cast things more canonically and use "fact quotes," $^f Sun's\ being\ large^f$, to indicate the fact related to (the fact known). But there is really no need to over canonize, when the use of nominalized forms like "the sun's being large" make the fact in question clearly available.[4]

As I remarked early in the chapter, it is not as if for Descartes there is, on top of the metaphysics of cognition (e.g., of thinking), quite another, to many of his readers prior, science—epistemology, the theory of normative justification of our thinkings. Not at all. On my reading of Descartes, for him there is only metaphysics through and through—there is the metaphysics of cognition of the sun (e.g., seeing it in broad daylight); with added invariants satisfied, we have the emergence of higher kinds of cognition, thinkings-of-the-sun; and with yet newer added invariants satisfied, we have at hand a certain kind of successful thinking of the sun, knowing-of-the-sun and its ways. It is all a matter of tracing how a certain kind of sun-thinking came about in me—when I think to myself that it is a planet and about to sink on the horizon into the ocean, one causal sequence of cosmic events, from the sun to Almog's mind, took place; when I think of its being a star or "my own" planet earth continuing to orbit round it, quite a different causal sequence of cosmic events, from sun to Almog's mind, took place.

When we sort the two sequences, how the sun and its ways brought about my thinking thereof, we would have the key: sometimes I have mere (false) thinkings of the sun, sometimes, as luck would have it, true thinkings of it that still make up no knowing of its ways; and sometimes true thinkings that do make genuine knowings of its ways.

Two Notions of Accidental Contact

We begin by harking back to Descartes' theory of thinking, the key to his theory of knowing. We need to remind ourselves of a certain key factor—the worldly basis—of the relation of thinking.

I am at a party, and you are in front of me, obviously drinking repeatedly from the martini glass you are holding. In fact, unbeknownst to me, you are drinking water. The only person in the party who is genuinely drinking a martini, Ferdinand, is away from my visual field, in the kitchen. Donnellan is convinced that when I say "The man drinking the martini is..." I refer to you and think about you. I have no thought about Ferdinand, even if he makes true/false my public language sentences. Truth, the satisfaction of a contentful condition, like the relation of Fregean denotation above in chapter 2, cannot, by itself, make me think about, have in mind, a worldly item. And so, given your pretense (you are absolutely not tipsy) and Ferdinand's serious intoxication, if I think to myself that the man drinking the martini is tipsy, I am thinking something false about you, not something true about Ferdinand.

I would like it noted that no amount of Kripke-like upgrading of the contentful condition by rigidifying the description—such as the man who actually is the only martini drinker in the party— is going to tip the scales. I am still thinking of whoever generated my thinking, that is, you, not of the denotation, whoever (and in all possible worlds) satisfies the contentful condition.

So much regards *thinking about*. I submit that a structurally similar proposal is made by Deacartes in the theory of knowing. Yet again, we need to bar a certain kind of accidental or even necessarily accidental relation between an agent and a worldly fact—as there was between me and kitchen-bound Ferdinand. If I, the agent, am to genuinely know the fact (and not have a mere justified true belief in it), the fact must *generate* my knowledge. It is not enough that it accidentally or necessarily-accidentally *correspond* to the fact. This generability thesis was originally suggested by Descartes in meditations III and VI. The point had been reformulated forty years ago, in a modern dress, and created a stir in recent epistemology under the heading of "Gettier cases." But the key lesson concerning the kind of relation—generative one—an agent needs to have with the world to be knowing the world's facts was already clear to Descartes. Let me then lay out in some detail the analogy between Gettier cases in the theory of knowing and Descartes' generative account of *thinking about*.[5]

Post-Gettier Fixings of the Accidental Connection

In our new Gettier party case, I think to myself "There's a (unique) tipsy martini drinker in the party." I have a belief here. It is true because, unavailable to me, Ferdinand is (uniquely) tipsily serving himself martinis in the kitchen. And if anybody was ever justified in a Gettier case, I am—given your explicitly tipsy-looking behavior in front of my eyes and my eyes solemnly keeping track of your behavior, I do have a justified belief. Do I know that there is tipsy martini drinker in the party? No, says Gettier.

It is often said the source of the trouble here is that my justified true belief is gotten accidentally. But two rather different notions of accident lurk in the wings. One is an analog of Kripke's idea of "accidental content"—my justified belief could have very well failed me—the belief I draw from looking at you only accidentally matches the truth-maker Ferdinand-fact in the kitchen. My perceptual belief might have very easily missed the essential fact—the Ferdinand-based truth needed for knowledge—that someone in the kitchen is indulging in martinis. And so, we think, there was no necessary connection between the evidence I used—drawn from you—and the truth-making fact—drawn from Ferdinand.

To remove this sense of accident, we may launch—in the Kripkean manner of looking for rigid conditions—the project of upgrading my justified belief so that it necessarily would match the relevant kitchen fact.

Descartes would have none of that. Let us suppose one could build up a justification profile that is contingency-free, by stipulating that it could only match Ferdinand's martini-drinking in the kitchen. By our hypothesis, we now do not have anymore the sense that our evidence *could* have failed us.[6]

Progress made? We still have no knowledge because we have no process which, starting in the kitchen, engenders in me the state of knowing the kitchen-based fact. And we don't have such a process because my thinking state (my belief, if we speak with Gettier) is not the effect of the fact taking place in the kitchen. I do not know whether Gettier himself would have analyzed the situation this way, or whether a variety of modern post-Gettier "causal" theorists of knowledge would have accepted this diagnosis. But on my reading of Descartes, this is his diagnosis. Necessarily justified belief is no solace. It is necessary for my knowing that it would be a cosmic effect of the fact-to-be-known.

For Descartes, upgrading the quality of the normative justification is idle. The only way to remove the "accident" is for the key fact to be entering my mind by means of an efficient causal process, to generate—historically bring about—my knowing. And so if any accident threatens my knowing, it is not the possibility that my belief won't match the kitchen fact—even if it did (and necessarily) match it, this would not induce knowledge. The accident/essence test that matters is whether my cognition (be it a thinking or a knowing) originated in the kitchen (assuming this is where the relevant fact lies). If this is the pertinent fact, only it could initiate a causal process making me know . . . it.

Very well, the originating fact is necessary for my knowing. But is it sufficient?

Sufficiency

In the analogous case, of reference and thinking about, Donnellan was quite clear that not any old causal chain will do. I remember conversations with him in which he lamented that probably much cosmic debris from Neptune did cross our brains before Le Verrier's investigations (and if not from Neptune, then from some other invisible but energy-producing heavenly body).

We might say this using Descartes' language of a second mode of being (being in the mind): informational impact in the brain of the detective is not enough to bring into being-in-the-mind this or that object. For a coming to being in the mind, registration by the mind is necessary.[7]

The same applies to Descartes' approach to knowing. Would Descartes say that I know that the (bent-seeming) stick in the water is straight just because the fact, the stick's being straight—call it the origin fact O—impinges on my perceptual system? After all, it is this key fact O that caused me to have the appearance of the stick's being bent. Perhaps then I know that O, that is, that the stick in the water is straight?

Descartes is very careful in his descriptions of such cases, and rightly so. He says that the tower in the distance seems round and the stick in the water seems bent. Furthermore, in a key paragraph in Meditation VI, he addresses the case of the (so-called) "secondary qualities" to tell us we do know that the tomato is red, even though how it seems to us is not at all how (does not resemble) the redness (that) is in the tomato. This last sentence was, of course, mine, not Descartes'. Here is what he says:[8]

> And from the fact that I perceive by my senses a great variety of colors, sounds, smells and tastes, as well as differences in heat, hardness and the like, I am correct in inferring that the bodies which are the source of these various sensory perceptions possess differences corresponding to them, though perhaps not resembling them.

On my reading, Descartes tells us that we do see that the tomato is red and that grass is green. And this much—the seeming or the sensation—is not just an "internal" going-on "inside" our minds, a pure quale or pure sensation. Far from it. The appearances (seemings) we get are correlated one-to-one—and necessarily so (and stronger yet, by their very nature)—with objective (light-based) features of the tomato and the grass. It is only because the tomato has physical feature R that I see a red-seeming object, and it is only because the grass has feature G, that I get the green-seeming image. In both cases, my image is (i) the effect of the objective feature, (ii) even if the way it appears to me is not resembling or matching the features R and G in the objects. For Descartes, what sensation S_R (the sensation of R) and sensation S_G (the sensation of G) have essential to them is not intrinsic resemblance to features R and G in objects, but rather the one-to-one structure-preserving correspondence with the physical features R and G.[9]

The structure-preservation principle is the key for Descartes. He says that I know that the tomato is red when its being R causes in me its appearance with S_R; I know that grass is green when the grass's being G causes in me its appearing with S_G. I would not be knowing that grass is green (and that the tomato is red) if the grass's being G caused in me its appearing with S_R (and the tomato's being R, in turn, induced it's appearing with S_G).[10]

Necessity versus Sufficiency of Efficient Contact

We have just encountered cases where the necessary condition for (perceptual) knowledge would hold—the key facts caused my cognitive state—but it is not sufficient for knowing. The causation did not take place in the right way: the way (mode) I have come to be cognitively in is not reflective in the structured one-to-one way of the feature of the fact that caused my cognitive state. And so, I do not know; I am merely caused to have an appearance of the tomato (or grass).

And so it goes for Descartes. I know that that the stick in the water is straight only if the key shape feature of the stick, the physical feature ST, causes it to appear to me with that correspondent sensation of S, S_{ST}. If it appears to me bent, if I get to have S_B, I do not know it to be straight. I do think of it but ascribe to it—in my seemings—wrongly its being bent (I here speak of those of us who mentally think and say, "It is bent," not those cautious enough to merely say, "It appears to me bent").

The same goes for knowings of the sun. Did Aristotle know that the earth was moving around it? After all, it was the pertinent fact, the earth's revolving around the sun, that caused Aristotle, one way or another, to say that "the sun turned around the earth." But though the fact impinged on Aristotle's mind, it didn't register in it in the right way—it didn't appear to Aristotle that the earth revolves around the sun.

Descartes and Donnellan end up very much together—the causal process is necessary but not sufficient for pertinent havings-in-mind (and, en route, they both agree that causality-free necessary matching conditions for belief are no substitute for the reverse flow, causal information transfer). Now, as for sufficiency, more is needed than sheer energy transfer. To have an object in mind, to think about it, proper attention is called for. This need not (and does not) mean that the thinker can provide basic predicates about the registered object. But the object, say the sun, can't just send neutrinos flashing through my brain. I must register the object.

This much concerned *thinking-about*. The same applies to Descartes' account of *knowing*. Now, the object to be had in mind is the full predicative fact of the sun's being very large or the stick's being straight. To have this kind of object in mind in the knowing way, I must be caused by it to think of it; and to think of it, I must register it. If I register it—the fact—as involving a coin-size feature of the sun, I have not registered it, the full fact that has *being-very-large* as its inbuilt property. I may have registered the sun all right, but not the sun's *being large*. To register this last in my mind while preserving its structure is to register the full fact—the sun's being large (an analogy: I cannot have a set theoretic pair in mind, an item whose nature [structure] is to have both x and y as members, while registering only x but not y as member).

And so it goes for Descartes. When it appears to me bent, I may have registered the stick in the water but not the full fact of the stick's being straight. If the appearances the fact caused in me preserve the structure of the fact proper, then I have registered the original (and originating) fact in a knowing way. To know perceptually the stick's being straight, it must cause in me its appearing straight.

In sum, I would say that Descartes' theory of knowing follows the pattern of his theory of thinking about. The key "flow" is not from mind, by way of beliefs (conditions) to matching objects (facts) but the other way round—the target objects (facts) initiate a process of information transfer. This much causation is necessary. Sufficiency comes with proper attention and registration of the information—that is, through induction in one's mind of a structure-preserving appearance-seeming.

Descartes' Linkage Thesis: Knowing for Certain versus Knowing a Priori

So much goes for Descartes' account of knowing, knowing *simpliciter*. The account has consequences for our qualifying the knowledge with "special" adjectival qualifiers: self-evident, a priori, certain. This brings us to the cluster of theses mentioned earlier, (E2)–(E4): Descartes does not allow that we know in a contact-free a priori way, any thing we do know; he does allow us to know for certain much of what we know and independently of sense experience some of what we know. These claims feed on one another.

The Varieties of Special Knowledge: Self-Evident, a Priori, and Certain Knowledge

In saying that Descartes has no place for the category of knowledge a priori, we must understand what we mean by "a priori knowledge" and this will call upon below a few annotations (regarding the very gloss of this much used notion).[11]

Annotation 1: A Priori Is a Technical Notion

First (and, in the end, most important), the notion is a technical notion of philosophical epistemology, not a pre philosophical notion of ordinary discourse. This contrasts with other epistemic notions we make use of. For example, the notion of being certain about some fact is a vernacular notion; so is the idea that things could or could not turn out otherwise. In a similar vein, the metaphysical notion of what something could have been or the idea that this or that fact is necessary are all common currency notions. Not so with the distinction between a priori and a posteriori knowledge or the (Kantian) distinction between analytic and synthetic truths. The latter are technical ideas defined (or, glossed) inside certain philosophical systems.

Annotation 2: No Apriority in Descartes

The notion of the a priori as we moderns have it, is not one deployed in Descartes' writings. Leibniz (in the few places I have checked) develops some early variant of our modern idea; Kant surely uses it (and provides what essentially is our modern notion); Frege used his own expanded version of the notion extensively; modern twentieth-century philosophy, as in the writings of Russell, Carnap, Quine, Kripke, and Kaplan, surely (i) assumed the idea of a priori knowledge as part of the basic philosophical vocabulary, and (ii) used it with a modern gloss based on Kant. Informed by this pervasive use, we tend to often hark back to Descartes as if he too were using this later language. It is thus that we describe him as believing the truths *Cogito* and *Sum* can (perhaps even, must) be known a priori; we thus describe him as stating that we have a priori knowledge of all geometric and arithmetic truths, such as that right triangles have the Pythagorean feature or that $2 + 3 = 5$.

This ex post facto ascription to Descartes of the Leibniz–Frege contact-free idea of a priori is ill-founded. Inasmuch as the phrase occurs in Descartes, it rather occurs with a premodern, perhaps medieval, meaning, where the title of a priori applies to arguments that are from general principles to specific results, whereas the title of "a posteriori" applies to arguments from specific facts back to covering general principles. Indeed, often this "ancient use" matches (correlates) with the distinction between (i) arguments from cause to effect and (ii) arguments from effect to cause.

*Annotation 3: Descartes as Content-
and Dicta-Free*

Third, and stronger yet, unlike the German tradition of Leibniz and Frege (let alone our modern Carnap–Kripke–Kaplan semantic tradition), Descartes is not busy classifying contentful dicta—truths, statements, sentences, propositions, judgments—into our modern categories of truth by reason (vs. truth by fact), analytic truth (vs. synthetic truth), logical truth (vs. nonlogical truth), a priori known truth (vs. a posteriori known truth). Descartes is simply not in the business of classifying dicta or thought-contents. He is interested in cosmic (nature's) facts—is this or that purported fact open to doubt? Am I as certain of the fact of my thinking as of the fact of my walking? Is my certainty in the fact of the triangle's angles having a sum of 180 angles or God's existing any different than my certainty in the facts of my having a body or my being in pain?

Descartes' focus is not dicta and in virtue of what-in-their-content they are true. Descartes' focus is things and their ways (the foregoing facts)—the numbers and the triangles and the conic sections and the elliptic curves, me and the stone and the sun and God, (i) what kind of entity each of the aforementioned is, and (ii) what do we know about such a (kind of) entity? His orientation is not de-dicto and de-content but de-object and de-ways of the object (de-facts about that object).

Annotation 4: What Is It for a Knowing to Be a Priori?

Two main glosses have dominated our use of the notion in the last three hundred years: (i) knowledge grounded independently of sense experience; (ii) knowledge whose ground is absolutely general. I call the first the *sense-free* notion, and I will call the second the *singularity-free* notion.

There are various ambiguous notions involved in these glosses, such as "independence," "generality," and so forth. In speaking of ambiguity, I think of at least two readings of the key notions, two ways I will contrast as (i) the intracosmic (also referred to "immanent") reading, and (ii) the transcendental reading. The two ways of understanding the key notions lead to two readings of the function of reason and, in turn, to the period's favorite "ism," "rationalism."

Let us attend to some key notions we use in these glosses. On the intra cosmic reading, when we say that a feature F is invariant, we mean: F is a feature of cosmic objects, borne by the objects, and, as we permute them, F keeps being had by them all. In like manner, when we say "independent of sense experience," we mean: invariant under all specific sense experiences had in the lifetime of a given being. The intra-cosmic meaning intended is: independent of which sense experience(s) one actually has. Similarly for the notion of "absolutely generality": we speak of a feature F that applies in full generality, to all existing things. Thus, no doubt there is a difference of kind between the true generalization "every man is a man" (for that matter, "every thing is self-identical") and the true generalization "every man lived less than 200 years" (for that matter, "everything came into existence less than 15 billion years ago"). Both kinds of generalizations concern—have as subjects—the same range of cosmic things. The difference lies in the ground—the kind of fact—making the predicate true of the fixed plurality of subjects. Thus, for example, it might be felt that "is less than 200 years old" is accidental, even if modally necessary of humans—it does not follow from what the subjects are. In contrast, "is a man" is grounded in the very essence of the subjects (is not an accidental but an essential necessity). Be the explanation as it may, what we explain is a feature of an intra-cosmic range of things, with a difference in kind of predicate borne. In this sense, it is a difference similar to the one between "Joseph is human" (for that matter, "is self-identical") and "Joseph is in Los Angeles." Both are true, both are true of Joseph; but the former's truth is due to what he is, the other merely to how he is.

Through and through, it is cosmic facts that we know, regarding Joseph, Mont Blanc, and so on, not a grammatical feature, a logical form, a sheer content, linguistic rule, and so forth. This much is true, with bells on, for "I exist" as well as "Joseph exists" (as well as "I think" and "Joseph thinks"). The subject thought of (known of) here is the intracosmic individual, and, regarding him, in the gerund form, what's taken notice of is Joseph's existing (and thinking). At no point is Descartes suggesting, as many moderns have, that what is known here is that some precosmic scheme, metalinguistic or semantical, as in " "I exist (think)" expresses a truth."

So much for the intracosmic readings of various key notions used in the glosses of "a priori." I do not believe these intra-cosmic glosses were those intended by Leibniz and Frege and by a host of twentieth-century philosophers of language. My understanding of Leibniz's truth of (and by) reason and Frege's a priori grounds, let alone Kripke's trick stipulation cases of apriority or Kaplan's truths in virtue of meaning relations (e.g., "I am here now") is that they offer an essentially transcendental basis. And as I understand Descartes, through and through in this work, he denies at the outset any notion of truth or fact that is hyper natural. There surely are features applying throughout nature; even if some are "accidental" universal facts, others are true throughout nature—invariant—in virtue of the very nature of nature (or God). Descartes is keen to delineate such infrastructural features. But none are prior for him, let alone independent of, the facts of nature. Nature (and God) is all there is.

One final observation. There is here a further question—much pondered by Descartes, Kant, and Burge—but, in my view, from the outset it concerns only intra-cosmic facts, known only by efficient causal contact within the cosmos. The question is whether we know any one of the facts by specific sense experiences ("observation") or whether we, intracosmic beings, are infused with these facts by less individual-experience-dependent sources. For example, how do I have in me the thinking (and knowing) "space exists" or "material things exist"?

Descartes speaks repeatedly of things we know innately or by means of "innate ideas." And it is clear from his discussion, in Meditation III (CSM II, 26–27) and VI (CSM II, 57) that such ideas—reminding ourselves to read this just the way we read the locution "idea of the sun"—are from man's own nature, rather than picked up, as he says, adventitiously.[12] But this kind of generative source for my thinking—my own nature—by no means makes the ideas nature-free. To the contrary—innate ideas are doubly nature dependent: they are nature-of-man dependent and they (as well as man's nature) are overall-nature-dependent. Certain invariant features of nature—in the language of chapter 5, cosmic thinking invariants—are wired into men as products of nature (this is what I called in chapter 1 Descartes' conception of man as a very telling—to the aliens—cosmic fossil). The more primal the invariant, the more recurring it is in nature, the more we expect it to show up in man's nature and, specifically, in the capacity of man to think of nature.

After Descartes, whether by way of recent empiricism or works such as Kripke's on the sensation of pain, we have come to think that the "internal" (be they sense data or pain qualia, etc.) items are less nature-bound (indeed, Kripke proclaims them strongly independent of—possibly in existence without—the existence of the brain). There are some who think that if my idea of red or of an elephant is adventitious, I depend on red and elephantine things out in nature to get going, whereas when my idea is "innate," I am nature-free.

This reasoning is anathema to Descartes. My adventitious ideas depend on the vicissitudes of my life in nature. My innate ideas are so deeply ingrained in nature—and consequently in man's nature—that no matter what life I come to have in nature, they will be part of my cognitive endowment.[13]

Epilogue: Knowledge-Optimism and the dissolution of Skepticism

For Descartes, unlike more modern philosophers, there is no categorical dichotomy between our knowing that snow is white and our knowing that $2 + 2 = 4$. Through and through, all we know are facts of nature. There is nothing else to know, no domain of prefabricated dicta-truths (be they reason or language or stipulation—fabricated). And so, if we test things by looking at Descartes' own "special cases"—mentioned late in Meditation I—we get a nature-bound uniform account of knowledge, none of which is a priori in the transcendental sense.

As we saw in chapter 4, when I think (and soon, know) that God (or nature as a whole) exists, I only think-and-know this by depending on contact with cosmic structure. When I think-and-know that $2 + 2 = 4$, I know this only because the fact, itself a product of the most general features of the extended universe, has impinged on me. When I think-and-know of myself that I exist and think, I only think and know this because I am in contact with this whole man, JA; this individual—me—is the object of whom I know that it exists and thinks. Last but not least, as we see in meditation VI (CSM II, 55), when I think-and-know that material things (in the plural) exist, it is only through contact with the material things of nature, by way of the material medium, that I come to have them in my mind and in the right way, the knowing way. Through and through, I know nature-facts only by way of efficient contact with nature—its objects and facts come into my mind, and in the right way. There is no other way (to think and know).

So, we conclude with Descartes' optimistic finale of his own Meditation VI—we succeed in thinking about and knowing much of nature. The one question remaining is this: how does this optimism square with the specter of skepticism, which is famously associated with Descartes' *Meditations?* It is to this notorious question that I turn at last.

I see Descartes as diagnosing flights *away* from nature as the original sin *en route* to skepticism. We vainly say to ourselves: we free thinkers could be thinking even if there was no nature to think of. Our thinking (as we fancy also for our *willing*) is absolutely free, unsubordinated to (i) the *existence* of nature and (ii) *material contact* with it. What Descartes proposes is undercutting our *folie de grandeur* (or rather, *de penseur*) over nature, our allegedly nature-free thinking capacity. Instead he will provide us with a dose of reality—a theory of thinking for the cavemen, the *nature-chained* beings we all actually are and are so by our very *essence* as thinking beings. To be a thinking being—which I essentially am—is to be a nature-thinking man.

What then is Descartes' opposite dose of natural realism? First, his realism urges that I have to be put in—or better, find by myself—my right *place* in nature. Finding my right place involves two complementary realizations. The first concerns what I am not, the second what I am.

There is first Descartes' key observation in Meditation III (CSM II, 33) that each of us is an incomplete, mere "finite substance." Descartes points to our *doubting* and *desiring*—indeed, recall the *drives* that reflect such doubts and desires; and we so doubt and desire, he says, only because we are not God and we lack the control we merely fantasize about.

The complementary observation is about what it is to be the finite substance that each of us is, including the way we are in nature's image (and, as he says to Burman, by "in the image" he means "similar in kind" of that larger all-embracing nature). If, as Descartes seems to believe, nature-as-a-whole is not itself God (its creator), then, furthermore, we are in His image and in nature's image.

For Descartes, it is essential that, like any real being, I, thinking-man JA, am part of nature, part of the total ordered system of created things, just like the sun and my dog. But I am also special. Not special in being half outside the cosmos (a miniaturized God). I am *totally* inside nature, all of me, human mind, body and being. This in-nature existence is nothing tragic to cry over, for there is nowhere else to be—I am inside the cosmos and that is the only *place* I could be in (there is not any other realm or kingdom of ideas or ends or after life to moonshine over).

I am an incomplete substance—not God, not even a miniaturized God, not even about my own thinking. I make mistakes—the phantom limbs, the stick in the water, the tower in the distance. But this much is part of the natural system devised, in nature and by nature, to deal with my life in that ordered system of created things. I see it as bent in the water but for a good reason—it is because my eye's processing of light is so sophisticated and this one little perturbation is worth it (else my seeing it as bent would, in time, go by the board, just as our ancestors' tail did). One has only to read Descartes' Meditation VI (CSM II, 57–61) on the phantom limb case and the drinker-dropsy case to see his appreciation of how the *local fallibility* of my cognitive system is part and parcel of its *overall reliability* (the swinging of the airplane's wings permitting it to go through the turbulence). Thus, Descartes offers us nature-based reliability and certainty by all means; but by the same means, nature-means, he offers us no efficient-contact free a priori warrants—our cheekily striving again for divine status—for our perceptual system (or mathematical reasonings, for that matter). Nature's structure and its consequent shaping of the structure of our own human nature puts us in a position to know—by deploying our very *nature*—that we respond well. We succeed in (i) thinking of and (ii) knowing nature. That is the "security" we get. But there is no extra, trans-natural, security to fantasize about. We are as *secure* as *we* could be (I believe Descartes held the same about our freedom of will: we are as *free* as *we* could be).

Descartes' sense is that all of the created-nature things belong together and each is as much stamped as the next one as "nature's item" (though he might put it by saying each thing is tagged "has a bit of God in it"). What to me is striking is not so much whether the extra tag ("has a bit of God in it") is correct or rather we should stick to "nature's item." What is striking is that every item is tagged the same way, but *among* the items there are nonetheless important *quality* distinctions.

Descartes says:[14]

OBJECTION. Could God not have created you and yet not have created you in His image?

REPLY. No. For it is an axiom, accepted and true, that "the effect is similar to the cause." God is the cause of my being; I am His effect, therefore I resemble Him.

OBJECTION. But a builder is the cause of a house and yet it does not resemble him.

REPLY. He is not the cause in the sense we are here giving to it. He does no more than apply active things to things that are passive; and his work therefore need not resemble him. The cause of which we are speaking is the *causa totalis*, the cause to which the very existence of things is due. Now a cause of this kind cannot produce anything not similar to itself. For since it is itself an existent and a substance and in producing something is calling this something into existence, that is to say is creating something where before there was nothing whatsoever (a mode of production proper only to God), this something must at least be an existent and a substance, and so thus at least be in the similitude and image of God.

OBJECTION. But if so a stone and all other things will be in the image of God.

REPLY. They too will have His image and similitude but very remote, exiguous and confused; whereas I, to whom God in creating me has given me more than to other things, am thereby the more in his image.

This contains, on behalf of Descartes, my own brand of Moorean response to skepticism—turning one's back on the abyss. Yes, thinking man is part of nature just as the stone is. But no, it is not *in kind* anything like the stone or the flower or the dog or the brute. What makes for the quality difference? Man's thinking. But what is that? Not some supernatural thinking-quantum (that'd be a sly escape from Plato's cave). Not at all. Thinking is a remarkable process precisely because at the same time (i) it is making creatures of nature like us be what we *distinctly* are, and yet (ii) thinking makes us *interact* with the rest of nature—have its objects in our minds—by a natural process.

I would like to emphasize one final time the modal contingency (fragility) of thinking man—man might not have existed—and yet his essentiality to nature as a whole. We may perhaps see this by attending to an analogy in the small, to a microcosm. Let our microcosm be an acorn. If we look at the acorn, we know full well that contingencies await its development. At any point, it might be destroyed or not develop into the blossoming tree in the garden. Nonetheless, the blossoming tree was very much *in principle* and *potentially* in the acorn. It is of the very nature of acorns—part of the very principles governing their being in nature—to turn into trees. I say the same for Descartes' view of the cosmos and its developing so as to have thinking men in it. At any one point, this kind of being, thinking man, might have failed to develop or to be sustained in existence. But it is in the *nature* of the cosmos—was right there *in* the early quarks and leptons and the emerging spatiotemporal manifold—that nature were to generate, in time, life forms, which, in turn, at later times, were to bring about the higher forms that the gorillas and the orcas make. And, not least, it was already right there at the beginning, part of the very nature of the cosmos, that it would go on to sustain processes that would lead into that distinct fact of cosmic life, what I called in chapter 1 Descartes' cosmological Archimedean point—the existence of thinking men.

All of this surely did not involve a secret second Big Bang (or a second divine intervention) halfway through, a few billion years after the original origin, whereby some "life quanta" were added to the mere quarks and leptons. And it surely did not involve yet a third secret Big Bang, whereby to the quarks and leptons and the secret life quanta (purportedly needed for the amoebas and the lizards) were added yet more hush-hush cogitative-quanta. It was all—thinking men included—right *in there* from the very origin. "In there," to borrow from Frege, not as bricks are in a house but as flowers are in the seeds.

Notes

1. In this book I rely on *The Philosophical Writings of Descartes*, volumes I–III, edited and translated by John Cottingham, Robert Stoothoff, and Dugald Murdoch (Cambridge: Cambridge University Press, 1984–91); they are abbreviated CSM I, CSM II, and CSM III. Also referred throughout this book is Descartes' *La Géométrie* (originally an appendix to the 1637 *Discours*), here used in the French edition (Paris: Jacques Gabbay, 1991).

2. Descartes explains his *separer pour mieux unifier* methodology in general and as applied to the mind/body problem very clearly in a letter to Gibieuf of 19 January 1642, in earlier letters to Regius of mid-December 1641 and January 1642 (see CSM III), and primarily in his arm/body model, explained to Arnauld in the fourth replies (CSM II, 160) and dissected in *WAI*.

3. The two pertinent quotes here are from Descartes' letter of 28 June 1643. They read in the original as follows:

(i) la notion de l'union que chacun éprouve toujours en soi-même sans philosopher; à savoir qu'il est une seule personne, qui a ensemble un corps et une pensée, lesquels sont de telle nature que cette pensée peut mouvoir le corps, et sentir les accidents qui lui arrivent.

(ii) et enfin, c'est en usant seulement de la vie et des conversations ordinaires, et en s'abstenant de méditer et d'étudier aux choses qui exercent l'imagination, qu'on apprend à concevoir l'union de l'âme et du corps.

In my own free translation, (i) "the notion of the union which everyone has in himself without philosophizing; everyone feels that he is single person with both body and thought so related by nature that the thought can move the body and feel the things which happen to it"; (ii) "finally, it is by relying on life and ordinary conversations, and by abstaining from meditating and studying things that exercise the imagination, that we learn how to conceive the union of mind and body."

4. CSM II, 56.

5. (This longish note broaches issues in Descartes' philosophy of mathematics. The philosophy-of-mind-only reader of Descartes may safely skip it.)

In my experience, both as a young kid in France and later as an adult, when someone is asked to explain what exactly from Descartes' ideas is targeted when something is qualified as *cartésien* ("Where, where in Descartes?" I would ask), the reply vaguely gestures to the *Géométrie* as the encapsulation of the ground-it-all architecture.

Let me point out that when I speak of "institutional France," I do not speak of its mathematical institutions but rather of its political-ideological self-concepts. For, as a matter of historical fact, Descartes is part of a most distinguished French mathematical *practice tradition*. The makers of the tradition themselves would probably trace the underlying common nature of them all to being simply each a *géomètre* (geometer). They would self-describe in this way in spite of the fact that each of them developed techniques of *associating* (but not reducing) geometric problems with algebraic, analytic, and topological methods. For these abstract methods are in turn to be understood by yet deeper geometrical analyses. Descartes is a paradigm of such a *géomètre*.

What the practitioners would simply call being a *géomètre*, I would rather characterize as a practice of *conjectural mathematics without borders*, a practice that shuns both (i) foundationalist reductions (be it to logic or to set theory, late nineteenth-century developments) and (ii) the related epistemology-driven idealistic casting of mathematics as unlike the sciences of nature, with mathematics *re*-formulated as nature purified, absolutely a priori, and self-evident.

An insightful nontechnical description of the French tradition of conjectural geometrized mathematics without borders comes across from a reading of Laurent Schwartz's *Un Mathematicien aux prises avec le siecle*, Odile Jacob, esp. chapter 6. Another such assessment, made by a figure different from Schwartz in both temperament and style, but much bent on tracing historical origins of (his own) modern ideas, is given by the number theorist Andre Weil. In the background of his fundamental *Foundations of Algebraic Geometry* he kept stressing that his new "language" was bringing out ideas (themes) of both Fermat and Descartes. He does this in a rather acidly critical review (dedicated to a comparison of Descartes and Fermat's methods): Andre Weil, "*The Mathematical Career of Pierre de Fermat*, by M. S. Mahoney," *Bulletin of the American Mathematical Society* 79 (1973): 1138–49. And he does it more directly and, for me, forcefully in his less anecdotal and more conceptual "Sur les origines de la géométrie algébrique," *Compositio Mathematica* 44, nos. 1–3 (1981): 395–406.

6. An elegant explanation of Descartes' attempt to deliver some of the most difficult problems articulated by Greek mathematics is given by R. P. Langlands in *The Practice of Mathematics*, Institute for Advanced Study Lectures 2000, as well as in his "Descartes or Fermat?" (lecture given at the Tata Institute, Bombay). I thank Langlands for a copy of the latter.

7. I here focus on one way of explaining such contentful representations, a way, in my view, best articulated by Frege's idea of a content as a *way-of-being-given* the worldly object, what he called a *sinn* (the canonical articulation is from 1892; the idea itself as old as the hills). As we will see in chapter 2, Descartes confronts another mediative model, resting on the idea of receiving a "form" from (the form / matter combination making) the worldly object. The two models differ, on which more in the next chapter, when we work on more "technical" details.

CHAPTER TWO

1. Meditation III, CSM II, 27, henceforth the *sun passage*.

2. A very clear articulation of the MF model, in the context of Descartes' reaction to it, is given in Paul Hoffman's work, especially "Direct Realism, Intentionality, and the Objective Being of Ideas," *Pacific Philosophical Quarterly* 83 (2002): 163–79.

3. Hoffman, "Direct Realism."

4. (A somewhat autobiographical note. The student of Descartes-only may skip it).

The modern trend just mentioned—associated with Kripke, Kaplan, Putnam, and Donnellan—has been called "direct reference," though, in my view, most of its developers have not really made the referring (let alone the thinking-about) *direct*. Now, quite apart from the present book, if the reader is interested, and Descartes notwithstanding, I explain—following Donnellan's ideas—what makes reference direct (and what does not), using my own modern terms, in "Is a Unified description of Language and Thought Possible?" (*Journal of Philosophy* [2005]).

I will be putting aside our (at least, my) immersion in this modern material from reference theory because I believe (i) Descartes had his own conceptual tools to describe my thinking about the sun, and (ii) in my view, his descriptions were *ahead* of the modern accounts associated with "direct reference." Under this last title, I have in mind descriptions such as those offered in Kripke's famous theory of "rigid designation" or the (Bertrand) Russell–Kaplan theory of expressing-and-thinking "singular propositions." Descartes' views about thinking involve no such *theoretical* baggage—no possible worlds, propositions, designators, intensions, and so forth. What is more, Descartes' views avoid a lot of neo-Fregean residues that I find in the just mentioned soi-disant direct reference theories. When possible, I will point out why I see Descartes as being ahead (and more Frege-liberated, if one can be liberated from something that was yet to happen) than our modern theories. But all in all, Descartes stands on his own and should be understood on his own terms (and the terms of our own, forever and ever, *ordinary* language), leaving aside any *rigid designators, singular propositions,* and other such.

Speaking "chronologically," I knew of direct reference theories before I read Descartes' Meditations III and VI thoroughly. But when I read these in the early 1990s, I saw that he is ahead of the sophisticated modern refutations of Frege. It was thus not hard to understand Descartes' content-free account of thinking-about, without falling back on the direct reference apparatus.

The one place where I attenuate this bracketing off of the modern is when it comes to the work of Keith Donnellan. For Donnellan's notion of *having* a *thing in mind,* though not distilled from Descartes, bears interesting connections to ideas of Descartes (and in my head, thinking about Descartes has been enriched by thinking about Donnellan and vice versa). I have often assigned to the class, as an annotation, the task of reading Donnellan's original paper as a way of making the students understand in simpler terms the present chapter's key notion of "objective reality of an idea of the sun." On which notion (and its connection to "having the sun in mind"), see more in the paragraphs immediately below.

Donnellan's key paper is "Reference and Definite Descriptions," *Philosophical Review* (1966) (reference to additional works follows below). As will become clear when we move from sheer thinking-about to knowing (and knowing a priori), a modern dispute between Donnellan and Kripke—can we think-about by sheer *denotation* (satisfaction of a condition) and may we thus know anything *singular* a priori—was in my view settled by Descartes (in 1641) in favor of Donnellan. This dispute will show time and again here, in the discussion in chapter 3, in chapter 4's account of thinking of God, and in our discussion of knowing (a priori) in chapter 6.

5. In terms made available by 1966 by Donnellan, Descartes deployed here two *referential* descriptions of the sun, neither of which strictly *denotes* it—neither of which has the sun as its *denotation* (satisfier).

6. CSM II, 74–75, henceforth the *one object, two modes passage*.

7. This generic, free-variable case will be of great use when we turn in chapter 5 to Descartes' thinking *invariants*, which are holding for *any* thinker whatsoever.

8. I am here attentive to *creative* work by man. For example, a Monet (Apelles) "portrait" of the sun may depend essentially on *that* painter's painting it. But if we put the modern electronic camera at a fixed position, to take a photo of the sun at 10 A.M., whether I press the button or a time mechanism does so may seem inessential. Descartes himself was very sensitive to these distinctions, as the 1642 Regius letter just quoted shows and as is further made clear in his discussion in the fifth replies (CSM II, 256) of (the painter) Apelles' essential contribution to his-painting. Still, the main point remains: whether in Apelles' *creative* thinking or in my own *merely receptive* thinking (I just image the sun), what makes our havings-in-mind what they are is the *sun's* generating the thinking act and the sun's coming to be in the mind (or in the painting).

9. I owe the form of the principle to David Kaplan, who used a similar form for quite a different purpose in his unpublished APA presidential address 2003 "De re Belief." This formulation (D) is related to Descartes' own third principle (to be quoted immediately below) the *to be conceived it must be caused* principle. As will become clearer in a few paragraphs, in reading (D), we will confront a "representationalist" reading of its content and in turn of Descartes, one that

is very common in contemporary philosophy of mind. See, again, for such a reading, Hoffman's clear exposition in "Direct Realism."

10. In contrast to Caterus, Arnauld understands Descartes perfectly and applies his principle (which Descartes applies only to reals like the sun, God, complex machines) all the way to thinking of sensed phenomena like cold (which Descartes thinks are unreal or at any rate not as real, merely secondary and merely sensed).

11. What I just called the *how come* question, Descartes sometimes calls the *why* question—why did I come to think of the sun (and not the moon). The quoted passage is from CSM II, 76, henceforth the *to be it must be caused passage.*

CHAPTER THREE

1. In discussing the representational role issue, I have been helped by David Kaplan (some years ago, when he was writing a paper called "De Re Belief," itself a revision of a modern classic on the matter called "Quantifying in" [see below]). I have also been challenged by Tyler Burge, both in conversation and through his writings (mentioned below), and more recently by discussions, in Italy, with Andrea Bianchi.

2. In particular, if there were no human minds, just brains, the point made below about the trace would hold just as well (and apply to brain-traces). Of course this "if" designates no real possibility because, by their very essence, if there are living human brains, there are human minds.

3. At least on all the sides I consider here, in particular Descartes and his "representationalist" interpreters. Of course, he did not use "photons" to analyze light but he did analyze *light.* For a crystalline example of such a representationalist reading of Descartes, see Paul Hoffman, "Direct Realism, Intentionality, and the Objective Being of Ideas," *Pacific Philosophical Quarterly* 83 (2002): 163–79.

4. "Neo-Kantian(ism)" is another one of those "isms" I am uneasy about. But, as uneasy as I may be, I see the tag as capturing a substantial unifying theme here. It is my hope the elaboration that follows partially justifies the use of the "ism" ("Neo-Kantianism"). See immediately below in the main text.

The modern paradigms I have studied (and will focus on here) of these representationalist views are Gottlob Frege, "Sense and Nominatum," in *Readings in Philosophical Analysis* (1949); and Bertrand Russell, *The*

Problems of Philosophy (1912), chapter 5. In spite of press to the contrary because of his use of the evocative term "acquaintance," Russell is a paradigm representationalist. Ubiquitous recent examples of representationalism (in my sense) that I have studied are Jerry Fodor, *The Language of Thought*, and especially Tyler Burge and David Kaplan. See Burge's "Five Theses about De Re States" (forthcoming in a volume in honor of David Kaplan edited by Paolo Leonardi and Joseph Almog), in which Burge summarizes thirty years of thinking about the theme. See also Burge's "Reply to Normore: Descartes and Anti-individualism," in *Reflections and Replies*, a volume in honor of Tyler Burge, ed. Hahn and Ramberg (Cambridge, Mass.: MIT Press). This second paper of Burge comes up for discussion in various contexts in the present book; see chapter 6. A modern classic that amplifies Russell's view (and defends it) is David Kaplan's "Quantifying In," in *Synthese* (1968), whose brand of "representationalism" also comes up repeatedly below. As mentioned earlier, I discuss Kaplan and Burge in a Descartes-free context in "Is a Unified description of Language and Thought Possible?" in *Journal of Philosophy* (2005). Here my focus is on Cartesian themes. I should say about the three modern authors just mentioned that (i) my qualification of them as "neo-Kantian" is my own (and may well engender in some of them a violent reaction), and (ii) their clear articulation of brands of representationalism has helped me understand what many modern readers find as an inevitable reading of Descartes. A fourth dissection, directly of Descartes though affected by contemporary philosophy of mind (in particular the three writers just mentioned) shows up in Hoffman's very instructive "Direct Realism."

    5. *The Problems of Philosophy*, chapter 5. Ubiquitous modern examples of insisting on a form of the condition, even if in a more relaxed form than Russell, appear in David Kaplan's work. See his "Quantifying In," and "Reading 'On Denoting' on its Centenary," *Mind* (2005). Two other thinkers who much emphasized the condition are Peter Strawson and Gareth Evans, who both saw the condition as critical and "Cartesian." See Strawson's *Individuals* (London: Routledge, 1959). (I do not refer the thinker to Evans's writings because although I remember him with much fondness—he was my teacher—I don't like the way his brilliant oral discussion is reflected in his popular posthumously published, but edited, writings on the matter).

    6. Many presuppose the view or assert it bluntly as a platitude. An example of one who takes the time to *explain* why the thesis must be

right is Tyler Burge; see "Reply to Normore" and "Five Theses on De Re States." Burge calls denying the thesis "crazy." Well, I deny it. But putting aside my own personal mental state, I propose here that Descartes denied it.

7. Descartes is very clear about this in the fourth replies (CSM II, 156–60; dissected in *WAI*).

8. It is ironic that various modern philosophies of mind, like Russell's on sense data or Kripke's on pain, are categorized as "Cartesian." More than anyone else (who is no reductionist about mind), Descartes held that it is the very *reality* of mental matters—pain, feeling heat but also imaginings, and all the way to thinkings—that makes it impossible to *know* them with the *completeness* open to the divine mind. We can achieve about them clear and distinct *perception*—-and note that *perception* it is in the end—and this provides *certainty*. But certainty for Descartes is not some high-minded oracular exhaustive ("perfect") knowledge. By Meditation VI, I am certain that I have two hands and a material body, that my mind and body are joined in a close union, that I am awake and not dreaming; I am also certain that God exists and that an infinite substance exists, but my knowledge of many of the foregoing matters is *essentially* incomplete. In any event, my being certain about what I have clearly and distinctly perceived is a far cry from (divine) omniscience. What this certainty comes down to I will discuss in the next chapter regarding our thinking of God, where a problem for our cognitive hold on God—the real contact dilemma—is developed. See also the discussion of non–a priori *certainty* in chapter 6.

9. Thus, 327 years before our modern razzmatazz of "twin earth" (Putnam's idea in 1968), Descartes noticed, here on earth and without hypothetical implausible assumptions about other duplicate planets, that in my very actual head, as a matter of *fact*, perceptual images underdetermine the objects thought of (or seen). In a similar vein, Descartes did not (and we do not) need to think—as Normore urges him—of a hypothetical "twin sun" in the hypothetical twin solar system; all he needed to do was *look*, with many other struck stargazers, at the "false sun" visible for him in Rome (in 1624) and other places. See C. Normore, "Descartes, Burge and Us" in Hahn and Ramberg, *Reflections and Replies.*

Of course, in other places in the *Meditations,* Meditation I and its evil demon, for example, Descartes himself seems to indulge in extravagant hypotheses. On the role of the evil demon and its dispensability as a tool, see the detailed discussion in chapter 6 on skeptical scenarios.

CHAPTER FOUR

1. I agree with Descartes that if only we understood our *successful* thinking of God, the other pieces would fall into place. The last sentence of this chapter aims to vindicate Descartes in this respect.

Writing about God's existence and our thinking of Him had seemed anachronistic to many of my friends, given what they take to be the advanced "technical" ("scientific") state of analytic philosophy. To the contrary, I say. Attending to nature as a whole and its relation to God can be done in a very robust and commonsensical way, a *naturalist's* way (*naturalist* not in the sense of a reductive *natural*-izer but rather the sense of the activity undertaken by a bird-watcher or stargazer).

2. The classification of the *from my thinking proof* as an existence-to-existence proof will shine brighter in a moment, when we realize that, for Descartes, the proof from my thinking of Him (my having Him in mind) is a proof from God's having one mode of *being* (in my mind) to his having another mode of *being* (in reality).

On a related matter. The standard appellation of the proof in V as "ontological" seems to me misleading, proceeding as it does from God's essence (true nature, concept, definition) to His being. All the proofs have, of course, an "ontological" *conclusion*. What matters (and differs) is the *kind* of premises they proceed from. Unless the very *existence* of the essence (true nature, etc.) is itself object-dependent, the proof in V is very different than those in III, which *start* in the cosmos with a real existential ("ontological") fact, be it my own existence or God's existence in my mind.

3. The argument I will dissect is given in Meditation III (CSM II, 31–33), and is further elucidated in the first replies (CSM II, 74–76), the second replies (CSM II, 96–100) "geometrically" (CSM II, 118), and the fourth replies (CSM II, 163–64). I also rely on the response in the *Conversations with Burman* (Adam's edition p. 38) on worldly things (me, a stone) being *made* in God's image, each of us cosmic products (organs) having God (or nature) in us. The same applies to passages late in Meditation III (CSM II, 35).

4. I would like to point out that in my view a formulation of the *believer's choice* dilemma is implicitly present in Kant's discussion (critique) of the cosmological argument; see B631–44 in *The Critique of Pure Reason*, trans. Norman Kemp Smith (London: Macmillan, 1929). Kant there notices that we may well be on our way to prove the existence

of a (some such or other) *necessary being* but that that being would not have been forced to have many of our desired attributes. It is at this point, Kant suspects, that we sneak into the cosmological argumentation a "logical virus," namely the ontological argument, with its key use of the concept of *Ens Realissimum*, which is meant to force, from that concept, the object proved to (i) not just be but (ii) be what we want it to (predicatively) be. I read Kant as warning us that we cannot have it here both ways. If we argue from the existence of an *object* (e.g., me) to that of another *object*, we may well have to give up our predicative control. If we prime predicative control and *start* from the *concept* of *Ens Realissimum* (start from the concept, not from the Ens itself), we cannot infer the existence of the *object*. This fundamental dilemma lurks in the back of Kant's summary of what he calls the "very strange" situation involved here and is articulated by him beautifully in B643–44 (the sections leading to this articulation, B631–39, explain where we sneak the predicative control into the cosmological argument). I hope to expand in print one day on Kant's anticipation of the present dilemma. I have so far speculated on it in a longish manuscript (written for teaching purposes) called "Kant on Thinking about God—an annotated reading of B621–B644." A less explicit anticipation of the hard choice pervades Rogers Albritton's unpublished "On the Idea of God" (where he reflects on Hume's critique rather than Kant's but formulates in his own words a similar hard choice).

5. I would not like to divert us here from Descartes by addressing "standard" (by now *presupposed*) critiques of his (indeed, of any kindred) argument for God's existence. But I believe these critiques are so much part of the lore by now that they must be addressed, if only to allow untainted comprehension of Descartes.

When I say "as good as any mathematical proof I know," I do not mean this hyperbolically. Quite the contrary. On my understanding—and surely on his truth (rather than formal-combinatorial proof) oriented understanding of mathematical proofs—any such proof is out to *preserve truth*. And for Descartes, if there were no God and the extended world he created, there would be no mathematical objects (and kinds) and the mathematical truths they make true (indeed, there would be no *truths*, mathematical or other, period). So let no lover of mathematical truth scoff at God's (and the extended world's) existence. For more on mathematical truths (and our proving them) and how our thoughts of God and the material world are revelatory of their basis, see chapters 5 and 6.

6. The linguistic question lurking here in the wings concerns a whole class of true reports without objectual truth-makers. Other examples are the treatment of true negative singular existentials like "Vulcan does not exist," true predications with empty subject terms, "Vulcan seemed to Leverrier to be near Mercury" and direct-object reports like "I worship Zeus," "Hob and Nob both fear (admire, think about, conceive of, etc.) Cruella" (Cruella is meant to be a "nonexistent" witch). The question is: must we sacrifice the subject-predicate (or subject-verb—object) vernacular grammar in order to stay within a robust ontology of real things only, if we are to account for the truth (conditions) of such reports?

As a philosopher of language, my answer on this class of questions has been no. The key has been offered here by Donnellan in his "Speaking of Nothing," *Phil. review* (1974). The false presupposition Donnellan unraveled is that to give the semantics of a language, to predict the correct truth values, we must assign *thought* (*propositional*)- *contents* to such sentences, whereby it would seem we need to posit propositions with unreal, merely possible, objects.

My response (inspired by Donnellan) is that the patent truth of these report sentences is a *reductio* of this assumption about the proper form of semantics—that to provide a semantics is to assign sentences *propositional* (*thought*) *contents*. "Vulcan does not exist" is patently true. But not because it expresses a singular *proposition* that is true. It does not. For what makes it true, see Donnellan, "Speaking of Nothing," and my amplification in "The Proper Form of Semantics," in *Descriptions and Beyond* (Oxford: Oxford University Press, 2004). The last-mentioned paper works a similar truth conditional account for cognitive attitude reports involving empty referential expressions.

7. This is true modulo one qualification regarding the *tense* of the conclusion. Strictly, I am so far, by the sheer *logic* of the reflection of the conditional (the very logic that would apply to the substitution of God or the sun by Aristotle), guaranteed only that God *existed*. But the true and desired conclusion does eventually follow—that God *exists*—with one more step, due to the nature of this specific object. I expand on this in chapter 5, in discussing the *invariants* of thinking and how thinking about God, the sun, and Aristotle differ. But at the moment, I follow Descartes' own exposition, and abstract from this qualification.

8. The first quote is from Meditation III (CSM II, 35), the amplification from the second replies (CSM II, 96). I call the two-tier quote the *whole force of the argument passage*.

9. *Naming and Necessity* (Harvard University Press, 1980), 23–4 and 156–57. I have written repeatedly on Kripke's remarks on unicorns in the last two decades (I found the remarks fundamental but could not quite fully understand what he intended by them). Indeed, I am afraid that every paper I have written in metaphysics is in one way or another a footnote to these remarks of Kripke's (156–57). For a late installment see "The Structure in Things," *Proceedings of the. Aristotelian Society* 103, no. 2 (January 2003). I now believe, as opposed to what I used to believe in the 1980s, that of the two interpretations mentioned below, Kripke meant the predicative-definitionalist reading, not the real being interpretation.

10. The structural predicate *seems* sufficient. Keith Donnellan was cunning enough to imagine two different physical elements (isotopes) that might show up with a similar structural atomic description. He then asks, which one is *the* element x? In my own work, I raise similar issues about structurally (and not just phenomenally) similar species that evolved independently on another planet. I even believe that such structural isomorphs that involve distinct kinds arise in actual (rather than hypothetical) mathematics. On my reading of Descartes' ground method, Descartes was never a structural definitionalist, not even about mathematical kinds.

11. *Conversations with Burman*, CSM III. Of course, in the "image of " does not mean here "resembles phenomenally." It means "emanating from and reflective in its nature of." See also Meditation III, CSM II, 35.

12. In his forthcoming book on the *Meditations*, John Carriero argues from God's nature to God's existence. But I believe he wishes to hold, at the same time, that (i) the nature is not merely a predicate content, and yet (ii) it is not *generated* by an object in nature. An analogy that may be suggestive is the notion of atomic structure (as in the periodic table), where many might think that the "structure" is not generated (precedes particles of the structure) and yet is not a sheer predicate (Keith Donnellan views atomic structures in this way). This may well suggest a notion of *form* that is not phenomenal, is structure-driven, but a notion that is nonetheless not generable by existents.

I continue to think the notion is essentially predicative and in the "definitionalist-structuralist" vein of the philosophy of mathematics— to be object x or structure S is to be whatever falls under the defining *form* (a set of defining *principles*, or propositions).

I do not think Descartes' God (or, for Descartes, any other *real* being) can be so given. The reality of any being, let alone the prime being, must emanate from its being (and *acting*) in nature, not from property-bearing or induced principles (axiomatic dicta). Property-bearing and principles satisfied merely reflect the being's existence and acting in nature. See the next section.

13. Before I give an answer to this, let me mention a third type of confusion discussed by Descartes and, in admirable clarity, by Arnauld in the fourth replies. It is intermediate between the objectual and the predicative confusions (CSM II, 163–64). Descartes tells us therein that we have a confused perception of *cold* (ness). We project into the object, say the ice, something that's merely a sensation of ours. In the ice, there is nothing that (is like, is identical with) coldness—to speak with modern physics, there is a certain molecular alignment in it and a certain rate of molecular motion, and so forth. This is not *how coldness feels*.

I note however that Descartes emphasizes in Meditation VI that even if (i) the sensation of cold in me and (ii) the sensation of whiteness in me are nothing *like* the coldness and whiteness in the ice, the sensations map one-to-one onto the differences in the properties in the object and thus *track* structure. (This last is often neglected in Descartes' account of "secondary qualities." On my reading, Descartes emphasizes how *unresembling* my internal feel is. But this is not to say my spectrum of feels performs no function of tracking objective differences in objective properties in the object). I return to this case of sensations (and whether they track realities) in detail in chapter 6.

14. I am using *person* interchangeably with *man*, just as Descartes does in his very interesting 1643 letter to Elizabeth (dissected at length in *WAI*), where, speaking of men, he says "each of us is a person with both body and thought...." (Recall the sentence quoted in the send-off remark at the end of the preface.) See CSM III.

15. I do not find every step of the way here unstoppable, but I do believe that the conception is natural: first, no efficient cosmic connection with me except via my body; then, no thinking of *that* body without thinking of the person whose body it is. This, of course, does not mean that you would recognize the body as Almog's in any old circumstance. But the object you do have in mind, JB, is, by its very *nature*, Almog's body, and you are connected in thinking, whether you know it or not, to the *man* Almog. This does not mean that in thinking of some entity *x* (e.g., JB), every old essential precondition of *x*'s *existence* (e.g., the

sperm and egg I came from) is something I am *thinking* of, have in my mind. I enlarge on this separation, among the existential preconditions for a given object *x*, in chapter 5, while discussing *the cosmological invariants* of thinking.

16. Speaking for myself here, I believe that Descartes is right to take us to be successful in thinking when we think of God (though predicatively wrong and inevitably so). I do believe that the causal step is correct—in thinking of God, we have nature as a whole in mind. But I do not understand how to proceed at the essentialist step—the idea that the cosmos (nature) is the universe *created* by God. When it comes to the essentialist step, I see in "schematic terms" what needs to be argued, but I cannot do better than that.

CHAPTER FIVE

1. We presuppose all too quickly that because the relation accounted for is not *kicking* or *thinking* but rather "knowing," justificatory norms must be involved and this takes us into the science of "epistemology." But Descartes does not presuppose this.

2. We enter here into "details" (on which our dear planetary life depends!); for example, were there means in 1969 to fully annihilate the planet (and not just life on it) by nuclear devices available to human beings? One often hears, in Hollywood films and in more serious discussions of the higher mathematics of cold war deterrence, that there were. But whether this was true in 1969 or not, the "theoretical" question ought to be clear.

3. See the letter to Gibieuf of 19 January 1642 (CSM III).

4. A very ubiquitous example regards standard reconstructions—in philosophical circles—of Descartes' work on mathematics. It has been common to read him as (i) embracing a platonistic ontology of mathematical essences (e.g., the *form* of triangles), and (ii) banishing the imagination and promoting the pure understanding as the cognitive faculty critical for *doing* mathematics. Both assumptions are, in my view, not only false but literally topsy-turvy: Descartes' ontology for his algebraic geometry is deeply embedded in the structure of the material world, and the imagination is a key faculty in his deeply visual and paratopological basic ideas (topological before their day; it was left to Leonard Euler and Felix Klein and Henri Poincaré to invent the theories his intuitions played with). See Eric Charpentier et al. (eds.), *L'heritage scientifique d'Henri*

Poincaré Belin, 2005. As mentioned in chapter 1, I regret having to leave Descartes' mathematics out of the present work. Shades of what I have in mind showed up in chapter 1 and will reappear in chapter 6. More has gone into in the separate essay "The cosmic ensemble," forthcoming in *Midwest Studies of Philosophy* (2007).

5. This important theme in Descartes—what is built into us by nature (rather than by sensory experience)—and how it differs from the standard (Leibniz–Frege) ideas of a priori knowledge is a topic explored in chapter 6.

I would like it noted that if, for the sake of the hypothesis, there *were* beings who could bypass—as means for thinking—the efficient causation information transfer and the cognizer's response to it, the activity in question would not be what Descartes would view as a *cognitive* activity. It is often suggested that angels, let alone God, could just bypass such material media transfer—God just put into his mind or an angel's mind (an idea of) the sun. It might even seem possible that he could—or should be able to—put this (idea of the) sun in this bypassing manner in my mind (Paul Hoffman has put this possibility to me in a forceful way). In response, I would only say that I don't see that Descartes allows even God such cognitive bypasses, for Himself, angels, or my mind. It is written into the causal axioms of Meditation III and the first and fourth replies that the formation of havings in mind (or formations of a sun-idea) *must* proceed by the efficient causal route, with the object itself and nothing but it—the sun—initiating the transfer. Were the ensuing transfer not that causal *process*, the result would not be a sun—idea. Descartes considers the hypothesis that God would put such an idea (or the material things) in my mind and would bypass the material things proper as the causal source. And he *disqualifies* the hypothesis (CSM II, 55). Correctly, I would add, for not even God could undo the essence of what it is for an idea (of *x*) to be and how *x* must causally engender it. God (or nature) does not set out this essence only to undo it later (by a "miracle," as it were). If this is what the *nature* of coming to have *x* in mind is—and by Descartes' light-of-nature it is—it is then in His nature not to force the un-doing of this specific nature. Natures are forever.

6. I contrast this with adopting an opposite theme—the invocation of the possibility (by many, as we have seen in chapters 2–4, actuality and even *necessity*) of orthogonal schemes—orthogonal cognitive-bond mechanisms—of cognitive bypasses. This may involve

(recalling chapter 2) (a) the RC content-scheme, that is, any of the aforementioned agents would be thinking of the sun in virtue of (i) primarily grasping a representational content which (ii) by itself, *denotes* (is satisfied by) the sun, or (b) the MF scheme, whereby I think of the sun, in virtue of (i) it itself being a combination of matter m and form f and (ii) my directly apprehending f. For the MF model see Paul Hoffman, "Direct Realism, Intentionality, and the Objective Being of Ideas," *Pacific Philosophical Quarterly* 83 (2002): 163–79.

CHAPTER SIX

1. In reading this chapter, I urge the reader to have before him Tyler Burge's very helpful "Reply to Normore: Descartes and Antiindividualism," in *Reflections and Replies,* ed. Hahn and Ramberg (Cambridge, Mass.: MIT Press), which is about Descartes, and "Frege on Apriority," reprinted in Burge's *Truth, Thought and Reason* (Oxford: Clarendon press, 2005), which is on the varieties of this tricky notion. I have found Burge's exposition of various modern writers (Leibniz, Kant, Frege) on the issue of "special knowledge" very rewarding. His approach to Descartes (on this count as on related matters) offers a very useful contrast to the manner in which I have tried to account for the basic theme of this book—Descartes' naturalistic approach to cognition. It may well be that what I call below Descartes' notion of structural-efficient knowledge is interestingly connected to (i) Burge's gloss of Kant's ideas regarding cognitions based on the form of spatio-temporal intuitions, while (ii) being orthogonal to the more influential varieties of apriority based on internal scannings of "de dicto contents," a cluster of pre efficient causality, logic-based notions that I see as emanating from both Frege and Leibniz (let alone the twentieth-century semantical tradition).

2. The tracing of the cognition to the agent's nature is Descartes' own language, both in the earlier *Regles sur la direction de l'esprit* (1628) and in the *Meditations,* both in III (CSM II, 27) and in VI (CSM II, 57). This last passage is very clear.

3. In "Descartes, Burge and Us," in *Reflections and Replies,* , ed. Hahn and Ramberg (Cambridge, Mass.: MIT Press), Normore develops such a position for Descartes—if it is the real objects with no predicative control that we have in mind, we are in for very little knowledge (and trapped by radical skepticism).

4. "Fact quotes" are designating facts following the way David Kaplan suggested in 1969 to use meaning quotes to designate meanings.

5. As mentioned, Donnellan's having-in-mind cases came up earlier, in chapters 2 and 3. Gettier's original cases were given in his "Is Knowledge Justified True Belief?" *Analysis* (1963).

6. The key passages here are not only Descartes' already dissected replies to Caterus (first replies, the "to be is to be caused passage" of chapters 2 and 3; see CSM II, 76) and to Arnauld (fourth replies, CSM II, 162–64) but also the discussion in Meditation VI of both (i) normal functioning of causal information processing and (ii) malfunctions of the processing, CSM II, 56–62, covering both visual-external object perception and color and pain perception. See also the remarks on the stick in the water in the sixth replies (CSM II, 295).

7. "Registration" by the mind does not mean "awareness" or "consciousness of," if the latter connotes articulability or transparency. Many of our beliefs might be unconscious, yet registered in our minds. Surely, Descartes did not assume beliefs are in one's mind only if transparently available.

8. CSM II, 56.

9. When I speak of the tomato's being red causing it to appear red to me, I mean just this. Let no one translate this for Descartes as if this speaking of its (the tomato's) appearing/seeming to me *F* means that I have a belief that it is *F*. Seemings (appearances) of objects are just that for Descartes, with no further commitment to (i) analyzing the seeming in terms of a belief, or, weaker yet, (ii) as if the seeming must imply a belief about the object that it appears *F* or is *F*. Seemings of the sun are seemings of *it* and nothing else.

10. It is Descartes' key idea that one-to-one structure preservation is not at all a guarantor of intrinsic similarity and often is built on non-similarity. Thus Social Security numbers allow a structure-preserving reflection of the domain of U.S. citizens, but numbers are anything but similar (intrinsically) to people. Pictures, which are more like people, would not be rich enough, in span, to reflect one-to-one the identity of people.

11. In discerning the variety of notions evoked by "a priori," I again urge the reader to have by his side Burge's "Frege on Apriority" in reading the present section. Burge explains the differences between Leibniz, Kant, and Frege vis-à-vis this notion and ponders, quite apart from history, whether distinct glosses of "a priori" are

genuinely equivalent. He also makes very interesting suggestions regarding the *Cogito*'s status.

12. Descartes mentions in Meditation III, as elsewhere, a third type of origin—fictive—for ideas, but this does not apply to our purportedly a priori cases.

13. I have come to think that among modern writers Burge is actually close to Descartes' conception of "known by my very nature and thus by informational contact with cosmic structure." I originally mistakenly believed him to prime a priori knowledge of the cosmic-contact-free character (of the kind I read in Leibniz and Frege), but came to see that I was wrong. Burge's paper on Descartes, "Reply to Normore," sets these matters out clearly.

14. *Conversations with Burman*, CSM III.

Index

A priori knowing, 85–86, 88–91, 111n.5
A priori, 85–86, 113n.11
Absolutely generality, 89
Accidental connection, 80–82
Accidental contact, 79–80
Accident/essence test, 82
Active form, 27
Activity-occurrence invariant, 73
Ambulo, 14
Analytical method, 11
Analytic truth, 87
Apriority, 77, 86–87
Apriority first, 76
Archimedean point
  cosmological, 15
  description of, 8–10
  epistemiological, 14
  hunt for, 14–15
Archimedes, 14–15
Architecture, 13
Aristotle, 55, 67
Associating, 98n.5
Attention, 84
Axioms
  self-evident, 12
  from theorems, 11–12

Banach–Tarski paradox, 3–4
Bearer of content, 38
Being
  in the mind, 82
  second mode of, 82

Believer's choice, the, 50, 105n.4
Body-mind separation, 70
Burge, Tyler, 38–39, 90, 104n.6, 112n.1
Butler, Joseph, 10

Cantor, Georg, 13
Cartesian philosophies, 104n.8
Cartesian, 12–13, 98n. 5
Caterus, 27–28, 32, 113n.6
Causal step, 60
Causal transmission, 59–60
Causation process, 30
Certainty, 77
Chimeras-thinking, 17
Cognition(s)
  description of, 69–71, 75–76
  metaphysics of, 78
  naturalistic approach to, 112n.1
Cognition-free proofs, 47
Cognitive agents, 70
Cognitive bond, 46
Cognitive faculties, 9
Cognitive life, 5
Cognitive media, 16–17
Cognitive scientist, 5
Confused perception, 109n.13
Conjectural geometrized mathematics,
  98n.5
Consciousness, 113n.7
Content-resemblance mechanism, 29
Content telescope, 30, 44
Content theories, 45

Cosmological Archimedean point, 15
Cosmological invariants
    knowing, 75–96
    thinking, 63–74, 90
Cosmology, 11–13
Creator theory, 58–59
Crypto representationalism, 38

Dedekind, Richard, 13
Definitive predicates, 50
Dependencies, 72–73
Desiring, 92–93
De-Sun, 26
Direct reference, 99n.4
Dirt exists, 13–14
Distinction, internal/external,
    16–18, 39
Dogs exist, 14
Donnellan, Keith, 25, 82, 84, 100n.4,
    107n.6
Doubting, 92–93
Dreaming of sirens, 16–17
Dualism, 6–7

Efficient-causation invariant, 66
Efficient causation mechanism, 29
Epistemiological Archimedean point,
    14–15
Epistemiological questions, 8–11
Epistemology, 63, 110n.16
Essence of God, 56–57
Essentialist step, 60–61, 67
Evil demon, 104n.9
Existence condition for thinking-acts,
    33
Existence of God, 47
Existence of nature, 70
Existential high risks of thinking, 45–46
External distinction, 16–18, 39
External world, 37, 44

Fabric of thinking, 71
Fact quotes, 78, 113n.4
Facts

definition of, 78
ontology of, 78
propositions vs., 3
Fallibility of cognitive system, 93
False predicative beliefs, 40
Fictive origin of ideas, 114n.12
Flies exist, 14
Foundationalist axiomatics, 12
Frege, Gottlob, 3, 12, 23, 25, 45, 99n. 7
Frege–Russell form, 25
From His essence proof, of God, 47
From my existence proof, of God, 47
From my thinking proof, of God, 47,
    105n.2

Generalizations, 89
General necessity thesis, 41
Generic-thinking invariants, 64
Gettier party case, 79–82
God
    essence of, 56–57
    existence of, 47
    I am thinking of God, 51
    man versus, 41–43, 93
    proof of, 47, 105n.2
    Real being and nothing but, 57–58
    thinking about, 47–61
    thinking by, 42, 103n.6
God exists, 48–50, 60, 66–67, 91,
    107n.7
Grade of reality, 29

Having a thing in mind, 100n.4
Havings-in-mind of this mind, 36
Hilbert, David, 13

I am thinking of God, 51
Idea of a thing, 43
Ideas
    Cartesian, 43
    fictive origin of, 114n.12
    identity of, 31
    innate, 90
    origin of, 31

Identity of ideas, 31
Identity theory, 58–59
If God doesn't exist, I am not thinking
    of Him, 47
If I think of God, then God exists,
    47–48
Indexed-content theories, 45
Individuation, 44
Inevitable thesis, 41
Informative identities, 3
Innate ideas, 90
Institutional France, 12–13, 98n.5
Instrumental means, 37
Integration without reduction, 5, 72
Integrative dualism, 7
Intellection, 21
Intermingled mind and body, 69
Internal/external distinction, 16–18, 39
Internal representation, 38
Internal representors, 22
Internal world, 44
Intracosmic reading, 88–89
Invariances, 63–64
Invariants
    activity-occurrence, 73
    efficient-causation, 66
    generic-thinking, 64
    object, 64–74
    object-existence, 73
    subject, 64–74
    subject-existence, 73
    thinking, 66
"Is thinking," 6
I think of God, 51–53, 57–58, 60

Kant, Emmanuel, 86–87, 90
Kaplan, David, 25, 38, 87, 101n.9,
    113n.4
Knowing, 75–96
    for certain, 85–86
    nature's facts, 76–77
    a priori, 85–86, 88–91
    as successful thinking, 77–79
    of the sun, 84

theory of, 79–80
Knowing-which, 40–43
Knowledge
    a priori, 86, 111n.5
    false predicative beliefs as, 40
    omniscient, 43
    partial, 43
    pessimism about, 77
    re-founding of, 10
Knowledge dualism, 76
Knowledge-optimism, 91–96
Kripke, Saul, 3, 25, 42, 53, 56, 81, 87, 90
Kronecker, Leopold, 13

Leibniz–Frege contact-free idea of a
    priori, 87, 89–90
Le soleil, 31, 36–37
Limitative result, 49–50
Limit cases of the mundane, 76
Logical truth, 87
Logical virus, 106n.4

Man
    creative work by, 101n.8
    fallibility of cognitive system of, 93
    God versus, 41–43, 93
    integration without reduction, 5
Mathematics, 98n.5, 110n.4
Matter-form model, 24, 99n.2, 112n.6
Mechanism of having in mind, 29
Mediative-content approach, 22
Mediative predicative models, 23–25
Mediative theory, 17
Meditation I, 9–10
Meditation II
    description of, 10–11
    mechanism of thinking, 18
    reflection conditionals, 46
Meditation III
    description of, 11
    reflection conditionals, 46
Meditation IV
    description of, 11
    subject-matter theorems from, 11

Meditations
    description of, 4
    order for reading of, 9, 11–12
Meditation V, 47
Meditation VI
    cosmological picture in, 71
    Descartes' thesis in, 76–77
    description of, 11
    God, 58
    reflection conditionals, 46
Men exist, 14
Mersenne, Marin, 13, 52
Metaphysical language, 7
Metaphysical questions, 8–11
Metaphysics, 63
Me-thinking-the sum, 51
Mind, object in, 85
Mind–body-man
    description of, 6–7
    differentiation of, 7
Mind-body separation, 70
Mind space, 30
Mind-traces, 35–36
Modal contingency of thinking man, 95
Modus ponens structure, 48–49, 65
My having an idea of the sun, 27–28
My thinking of the sun, 27, 69

Natural realism, 92
Natural scientist, 5
Nature
    created-nature things, 94
    thinking about, 4, 92
    thinking-man in, 4
Nature-as-a-whole, 58–61
Nature's facts, 76–77
Nature-theorems, 12–14
Neat-thinker if and only if omniscient-
    thinker bi-conditional, 42
Neo-Kantian(ism), 101n.4
No mentation without inculcation, 32–33
No mentation without representation, 38
Nonlogical truth, 87
Normative Cartesian epistemology, 75

Object
    attention of, 84
    existence of, 106n.4
    in mind, 85
    way-of-being-given, 99n.7
Object-existence invariant, 73
Object-invariants, 64–74
Objects-of-thinking, 21, 68, 71
Objectual-thinking, 15
Omniscient knowledge, 43
One object, two modes of being prin-
    ciple, 25–29, 35
Ontological conclusion, 105n.2
Ontology
    of facts, 78
    of target objects, 24
    of ultimate objects, 24
Origin of ideas, 31
Orthogonal schemes, 111n.16

Partial knowledge, 43
Perception, 104n.8
Perceptual images, 44
Percipio, 14
Phenomenal profile, 40
Phrase soleil, 31, 36
Predicating of objects, 43
Predicative content, 22–23, 26, 39, 42,
    54, 74
Predicative definitionalist, 54–57
Predicative high risks of thinking,
    45–46
Predicative profiles, 26, 40
Predicative representationalism, 41
Predicative telescope model, 25–26
Preservation of reality, 29
Propositions
    description of, 3, 108n.12
    facts vs., 3
Putnam, Hillary, 25

Rationalism, 88
Real being and nothing but, 57–58
Real-love, 50

Reconstructionist foundationalist, 13
Reduction, 72
Reflection arguments, 65–66, 75
Reflection conditionals, 46–48, 112n.6
Re-founding of knowledge, 10
Regressive axiomatics, 12
Representational content model
    description of, 24
    variant of, 25
Representationalism
    description of, 38–40, 101n.9, 103n.6
    predicative, 41
Representational role, 35, 37–38, 102n.1
Respiro, 14
Rigid designation, 100n.4
Russell, Bertrand, 12, 40, 87, 102n.4,
    103n.5

Secondary qualities, 83
Second mode of being, 82
Self-evident axioms, 12
Self-evident thought, 14, 18
Sense-free notion, 88
Separatist dualism, 6
Separer pour mieux unifier methodology,
    6, 97n.2
Singularity-free notion, 88
Singular propositions, 100n.4
Sinn, 99n.7
Sirens-thinking, 16–17
Skeptical cases
    meaning of, 15
    questions about, 8, 10
Skepticism
    description of, 10
    dissolution of, 91–96
    illusory character of, 15
    metaphysical thesis, 17
Soul-analysis, 5
Specific necessity thesis, 41
Specific things, 22
Structural predicate, 108n.10
Structure preservation, 83, 113n.10
Subject-existence invariant, 73

Subject-invariants, 64–74
Sufficiency of efficient contact
    description of, 82–83
    necessity vs., 84–85
Sun exists, 66–67
Sun in my mind, 18
Sun-thinking, 67, 79
Sun-trace, 35
Synthetic method, 12
Synthetic truth, 87

Theorems
    axioms from, 11–12
    nature-theorems, 12
    subject-matter, 11
Theoretical organization, 37
Theoretical profile, 40
Thinking
    about nature, 4, 92
    cosmological invariants of, 110n.15
    definition of, 8–11, 95
    existential high risks of, 45–46
    fabric of, 71
    by God, 42, 103n.6
    mechanism of, 18, 28
    metaphysical, 17
    objects-of-thinking, 21, 68, 71
    predicative high risks of, 45–46
    questions about, 4–5
    sirens-thinking, 16–17
    of specific things, 22
    success in, 15
    unnatural nature of, 18–19
    unsubordinated, 92
    ways of, 42
Thinking about
    cosmic invariants of, 63–65
    description of, 40–43, 80, 85
    structural features of, 63
Thinking about God, 47–61
Thinking about the sun
    causal activator of, 32
    internal representors, 22
    principles of, 22–33

Thinking-acts
  description of, 5–6
  existence condition for, 33
  individuation question about, 44
  specificity of, 44
Thinking-fact, 27
Thinking-invariants, 66
Thinking man
  interpretive question about, 8
  modal contingency of, 95
  in nature, 4
  paradox, 3–19
  textual issue about, 8–9
Thinking of the sun, 64, 74
Thinking-of-triangles, 32
Thinking premise, 48
Thinkings, 44
Thinkings-of-the sun, 79
Thought-free proofs, 47

To be conceived it must be caused, 32–33, 101n.9
Trace-fabric question, 35–37
Transcendental reading, 88, 90
Triangles, 32, 71, 110n.4
Truth by reason, 87

Unicorns, 53–54, 56, 108n.9
Unsubordinated thinking, 92

Way-of-being-given, 99n.7
Ways of thinking, 42
Weber, Heinrich, 13
Weil, Andrew, 99n.5
What Am I?
  definition of, 4
  separatist dualism, 6
World, The, 30–31

Zermelo, Ernst, 12